WANTED: ONE FREUDIAN SLIP

By the same author and published by Robson Books:

Written in Jest

WANTED: ONE FREUDIAN SLIP

AND ALL OTHER ODD ITEMS CONSIDERED

MICHAEL A. LEE

(aka The Beast of Bodmin Moor)

ROBSON BOOKS

First published in Great Britain in 2003 by Robson Books, The Chrysalis Building,
Bramley Road, London, W10 6SP

An imprint of **Chrysalis** Books Group plc

The author has made every reasonable effort to contact all copyright holders. Any errors that may have occurred
are inadvertent and anyone who for any reason has not been contacted is invited to write to the publishers so
that a full acknowledgement may be made in subsequent editions of this work.

British Library Cataloguing in Publication Data
A catalogue record for this book is available from the British Library.

ISBN 1 86105 680 X

Typeset by SX Composing DTP, Rayleigh, Essex
Printed by Butler & Tanner Ltd, Frome and London

To my ever-patient wife, Ann-Marie,
and my two wonderful sons,
Tom and George

INTRODUCTION

As many of you doubtless will already know – if you have read or heard about my first book, *Written in Jest* – I am 'The Officially Recognised Beast of Bodmin Moor' and am very proud of this auspicious title. Having applied for a variety of roles and positions, including Principal Stable Boy for the Four Horses of the Apocalypse, Jack the Giant Killer, and Government Scapegoat, I was eventually offered a colourful contract by a group of refreshingly creative and insightful Cornish business people permitting me to roam the moors, growl whenever I feel fit and to help myself to the local mice.

Since receiving this freedom of the hills in 2002 I have indeed roamed the moors on many occasions, growled for varying periods of time and at a host of individuals, and have gone as far as to consider a diet of mice. (To be frank, I have generally chosen a more familiar diet of lamb chops or chicken whenever possible, but feel particularly beastly as a consequence.) After several weeks of enjoying the novelty of my beastliness I decided to begin writing once again to a range of individuals, but this time in a purposeful quest for unusual items. Surely The Officially Recognised Beast of Bodmin Moor, a most unusual creature indeed, deserves to acquire items and products that are themselves rather unusual?

And so it began. In response to a host of letters to Next requesting a 'Freudian Slip' for my wife's birthday present, to Wilkinson for a 'corporate ladder' to further my career progression, and to Battersea Dogs Home for 'a hair of the dog' for my hangovers – to name but a few – replies began to flood in. Wonderful epistles full of enjoyable wordplay, lateral thinking and quirky communication mixed with humour and *joie de vivre* were sent from such highly regarded people as Lord Harewood, the Archbishop of York and Frank O'Dwyer of Huddersfield. Similarly, countless (unless you cared to count them of course) examples of wit and goodwill were compiled by those working for large organisations such as Boots, Nestlé and, once again, MI5. Indeed, the aristocracy, those from the worlds of medicine and law, men of the church and corporate life-servers were all invited by pen (actually, word processor) to involve themselves in an anthology of light-heartedness just across the border from convention and the mundane. Many took up the challenge and here are the results.

I predict that you will either smile with pleasure or cry with laughter as you read the following pages. I believe many of you will attempt to compile a list of items you would have requested, not included herein. Most of you will doubtless sit down to read this book though, of course, if you would prefer a 'long stand' instead that is entirely your business . . .

Customer Service Manager
Next Retail Ltd
Desford Road
Enderby
Leicester LE19 4AT

Dear Sir/Madam

I am writing to you as part of my quest for an unusual item; namely a pretty 'Freudian Slip' for my wife.

Only last week my wife and I threw a dinner party here at our home in Huddersfield and enjoyed a wonderful meal along with several glasses of wine with some friends. The conversation was varied and delightful and we touched on areas as diverse as psychology and lingerie.

It was during this relaxed and stimulating conversation that I seem to recall one of my friends saying he had purchased a Freudian Slip for his wife and it occurred to me afterwards that a similar gift might well also provide an excellent present for my own wife on the occasion of her next birthday.

In this regard I wondered, as a national retailer of ladies and gentlemen's fashion, if you might be able to advise me with reference to the styles and colours of slips you sell and whether any of them carry the Freudian brand name. In asking for such advice may I say that my wife is almost 41 years old and therefore not such a Jungian as she used to be and so a reasonably conservative style of slip would be more appropriate than something too obviously suggestive.

Many thanks indeed for your time and kind consideration in this matter and I look forward to hearing from you in the very near future.

Sincerely

M. A. Lee

Michael A. Lee

NEXT

Customer Service Department
Desford Road, Enderby, Leicester, LE19 4AT

Our Ref:2048664/PE
09 April 2002

Mr M A Lee
Somewhere in West Yorkshire

Dear Mr Lee,

Thank you for your recent letter, which has been forwarded for my attention by the Customer Service Manager, requesting advice on where to obtain a 'Freudian Slip' for your wife's Birthday present.

Our Lingerie Department stocks a stunning Black Slip M41669 for £19.99, which perfectly fits the requirements stated in your letter and is both sexy and sophisticated.

Alternatively I have the details of three very pretty and becoming Jersey Slips from our Spring/Summer 2002 Nightwear range. These are:

M37435	Blue 'Cheeky Devil' Slip	£14.99
M37437	Pink Jersey Slip	£16.99
M52816	Lilac Embroidered Woven Slip	£16.99

I have forwarded a copy of your letter to our Ladieswear Product Director for her future reference and consideration. Your interesting comments will be greatly appreciated when considering future ranges for our Ladieswear Lingerie Selection. I am sure she will endeavour to investigate the Freudian Brand Name further, as this is a Nietzsche of the market we are currently looking to expand.

Thank you for taking the time and trouble to write to us concerning this matter. Next considers customer feedback to be essential in helping to improve our goods and services. I hope this information has been of some assistance.

Yours sincerely,

Portia D Edmiston
Customer Services Department

Contact Customer Services on 0870 243 5435. Our opening hours are 9.00am - 5.30pm Monday to Saturday; 11.00am - 5.00pm Sundays. Fax: 0116 284 2318   E Mail: enquiries@next.co.uk.

NEXT RETAIL LTD. DESFORD ROAD, ENDERBY, LEICESTER, LE19 4AT. TELEPHONE: 0116-286 6411
TELEX 34415 NEXT G. FACSIMILE: 0116 284 8998.

REGISTERED IN ENGLAND 123434. REGISTERED OFFICE, DESFORD ROAD, ENDERBY, LEICESTER LE19 4AT.

0104

3

Somewhere in West Yorkshire
14 June 2002

Portia D. Edmiston
Customer Services Department
Next Retail Ltd
Desford Road
Enderby
Leicester LE19 4AT

Dear Portia

First and foremost may I thank you for your response dated 9 April 2002 to my letter enquiring about the acquisition of a Freudian Slip for my wife. Your recommendation of various items was enormously helpful. I was pleased also to hear that the Ladieswear Product Director will look further at the Freudian brand name and indeed plans to exploit fully the opportunities within this Nietzsche of the market. I trust that the range will be sold at prices that do not convince your customers to Hegel!

Since you were so helpful previously I wondered if I might once again ask your advice regarding another acquisition; that of a shirt which changes colour according to its surroundings.

As an avid viewer of TV programmes connected with wildlife, I recently watched with great interest and enthusiasm a documentary concerning animals such as the chameleon and the squid that have the ability to change colour and patterning according to the environment. I cannot specifically remember how many variations of colour, shade and patterning were involved in the case of these creatures but it was certainly comprehensive, to say the least, and offered them camouflage when required as well as a means of efficient communication. These reptiles and beasts of the oceans literally make biological fashion statements. Although I assume that the acquisition of a shirt that mimics the versatility of the skins of the aforementioned species will involve significant expenditure, I would be more than willing to spend my hard-earned cash on such an item as a long-term clothing investment. Furthermore, as you are a large, established purveyor of items such as men's shirts whose range is deemed to be of the highest calibre with an admirable variety, I have no doubts that you will be more than able to help me in my enquiries.

I would indeed be proud to experience my shirt changing rapidly from a shade of grass green whilst I mow the lawn to a blue, mauve and sunshine-yellow patchwork as I step into my tasteful utility room for a cooling drink. I could blend into the background if faced with a threatening situation by adopting a pebbledash shirt effect against a nearby house wall or present myself as a dynamic individual by changing my shirt colour to one that contrasts in a bright and even gaudy fashion with the bland and grey shades and hues adjacent to it. It is with great amazement that I look at the many developments of our 21st-century hi-tech world and with great anticipation that I look forward to wearing a shirt of this type with an incredible and obvious difference.

Many thanks indeed for your time and kind consideration in this matter and I look forward to receiving any advice you believe will be helpful in my search for the above garment.

Sincerely

M. A. Lee

Michael A. Lee

NEXT

Customer Service Department
Desford Road, Enderby, Leicester, LE19 4AT

Our Ref:2048664/PE
17 June 2002

Mr M A Lee
Somewhere in West Yorkshire

Dear Mr Lee,

Thank you for your very interesting letter. I was very impressed that so much contemplation has gone into formulating the fantastic idea that you have presented.

Shirts such as you describe would certainly put Next at the cutting edge of modern fashion. It could lead to a whole new dimension of colour coding as we know it. For example, our Home department could produce sofas and curtains that change colour to co-ordinate with different people as they enter the room depending on what mood they are in. The possibilities of this idea are limitless and I would therefore like to thank you for writing in with your suggestions.

I have passed a copy of your letter to our Menswear Product Director and hopefully, being a man of reason and integrity, he will see what he can do about transforming your dreams to reality. Please be assured that when the first phase of ChaMichael A Leeleon Shirts are released onto the market, you will be rewarded for your inspiration. Next, as an ethical retailer, will not forget your hand in our future success.

In the meantime, the following Men's shirts are extremely comfortable and change colour slightly when you squint your eyes. They are part of our Autumn/Winter 2002 range and will be available from the middle of August:

M70517 Soft Touch Microcheck Shirt £19.99 short and long sleeves available in 4 colours
M23710 Long Sleeve Soft Touch Textured Shirt £26.00 available in 5 colours

Thank you for another thought-provoking letter. Please rest assured that you will be the first to know if I happen to discover that these shirts have already been made. Until that time, I wish you a great deal of sunshine to assist your gardening exploits. It was lovely to hear from you again.

Yours sincerely,

Portia D Edmiston
Customer Service Department

Contact Customer Services on 0870 243 5435. Our opening hours are 9.00am - 5.30pm Monday to Saturday; 11.00am - 5.00pm Sundays. Fax: 0116 284 2318 E Mail: enquiries@next.co.uk.

Somewhere in West Yorkshire
8 April 2002

Head of Geography
Durham University
Durham
County Durham

Dear Sir/Madam

I am writing to you as part of my quest for an unusual item; namely details about a place I have heard mentioned many times over the last 40 years or so but about which I can find little in the way of concrete geographical information. I cannot even locate it in my world atlas. The place to which I allude is none other than Cloud Cuckoo Land!

It is with a sense of wasted time and effort that I must tell you of my many hours and perhaps days spent searching in a keen yet futile manner for further information about this intriguing place in libraries, on the Internet and in countless bookshops. I have searched high and low for further knowledge about a land I would love to visit and explore but which seems to elude even the greatest minds in the worlds of geography, travel and anthropology.

Even some of the better-known High Street travel agents were unable to help in my desperate search, although they did manage to mention their cut-price travel insurance during their feeble attempts.

It is for this reason that I decided to approach an institution regarded as one of England's finest as far as academia and learning is concerned: Durham University and its world-famous Department of Geography.

Doubtless there have been many other men and women of curious and searching minds who have also approached you for some clues regarding the whereabouts of Cloud Cuckoo Land and I am proud to join their ranks. In this regard I would be most grateful for any advice you can provide and I look forward to hearing from you in the very near future.

Sincerely

M. A. Lee

Michael A. Lee

University of Durham

Department of Geography

Science Laboratories
South Road
Durham DH1 3LE, UK
Fax: **0191 374 7307**
Direct Line: **0191 374 2458**
E-mail: **R.J.Allison@durham.ac.uk**

187.02

12th April 2002

Mr M A Lee
Somewhere in West Yorkshire

Professor Robert J. Allison B.A., Ph.D.
Chairman of the Board of Studies

Dear Mr Lee

Cloud Cuckoo Land

Thank you for your letter dated 8th April 2002.

I suspect that you may be looking in the wrong sources. Rather than searching for an answer to your query in an atlas, please refer to the Oxford Companion to English Literature. The attached may be of interest.

Yours sincerely

Professor Robert J. Allison
Chairman of the Board of Studies

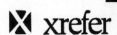 | select a topic | | GO Help

xreferences

Aristophanes (c. 448 - 380 bc)
The Oxford Companion to English Literature

adjacent entries

Clorin
Clorinda
Cloten
Cloud-cuckoo-land
Cloud of Unknowing, The
Clough, Arthur Hugh (1819 - 1861)
Club, The

Cloud-cuckoo-land

(Nephelococcygia), an imaginary city built in the air in *The Birds* of Aristophar

The Oxford Companion to English Literature, © Margaret Drabble and Oxforc 1995 ⓘ

Home | About | Feedback | Help
Title List | Testimonials | Add xrefer to your browser | Add xrefer to your site
© 2002 xrefer | Privacy

Somewhere in West Yorkshire
8 April 2002

The Director
RSPB HQ
The Lodge
Sandy
Bedfordshire SG19 2DL

Dear Sir/Madam

I am writing to you as part of my quest for an unusual item; namely some information about a particular type of bird I heard about whilst flicking from channel to channel on NTL cable television last week.

For many years now I have been a keen amateur ornithologist and have a reasonable though not exhaustive knowledge of birds both in the UK and from around the world but I had never before heard of a 'Culture Vulture' until my semi-concurrent Friday-evening viewing of the 'Animal Planet' and 'Discovery' channels, and the programme 'Frazier'. Indeed, for a moment or two I actually thought I might have been a little confused!

I seem to remember that this particular type of vulture is a cut above the rest when it comes to vultures generally and enjoys a range of more select food than its less fussy cousins. It prides itself on a nicely groomed appearance and enjoys observing with a critical eye the theatrical comings and goings of other birds and animals on the stage of its tropical home. In addition to these facets of behaviour, its cry is more refined than that of other birds and it hops in a way suggestive of particularly good breeding and class.

I would be most grateful if you could provide me with any other details you have regarding this strange and interesting bird and I look forward to hearing from you in the very near future. I thank you for your time and consideration but really must fly.

Sincerely

Michael A. Lee

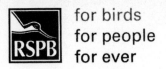 **RSPB**

for birds
for people
for ever

UK Headquarters
The Lodge, Sandy
Bedfordshire SG19 2DL
Tel: 01767 680551
Fax: 01767 692365
DX 47804 SANDY
www.rspb.org.uk

12/4/02

Dear Mr Lee,

Thank you for your letter dated 8/4/02.

I am not so sure what to make of your letter but in general terms, this is indeed true of all species of birds. There is always one individual that is in someway different (I hesitate to use the word superior). These individuals tend to be the most successful in attracting mates and competing for food. I should add that appearance is not always the defining characteristic so much as strength. I had to smile a little at the reference for your information and without wishing to be critical; it is typical of the Americans to coin an anthropomorphic term to label this with.

Anyway, I certainly do not want to be picking over the bones of this subject because it is a bit of a soar point. You can groan now!

Yours sincerely

Ian Peters

 BirdLife
INTERNATIONAL

Patron Her Majesty the Queen **President** Jonathan Dimbleby **Chairman of Council** John Croxall **Chief Executive** Graham Wynne

Registered charity no 207076

Somewhere in West Yorkshire
25 April 2002

Ian Peters
RSPB
UK Headquarters
The Lodge
Sandy
Bedfordshire SG19 2DL

Dear Mr Peters

First and foremost I would like to thank you for taking the time and effort to reply to my letter asking for advice about the 'Culture Vulture'. Armed with the information you sent to me I have now begun asking various travel agents whether they might organise a reasonably priced holiday for me so that I might visit the natural habitat of these creatures in a bird-watching and photographic capacity. I am looking forward to the trip with great excitement and a sense of the 'unknown'!

Inspired by this recent addition to my knowledge about our feathered friends, I turned on my TV again last night and to my astonishment heard the phrase 'pigeon's milk' in reference, I believe, to nutritional foods. (I was at the time channel hopping between 'Animal Planet' and a cookery programme.)

I wonder in this regard whether you might be able to advise me of any retail outlets in the North of England that specialise in the sale and supply of 'pigeon's milk' and whether you know anything of its packaging in terms of volume or of the availability of full cream, semi-skimmed and fat-free varieties.

Once again I thank you for your time and kind consideration and look forward to hearing from you in the very near future.

Sincerely

Michael A. Lee

for birds
for people
for ever

UK Headquarters
The Lodge, Sandy
Bedfordshire SG19 2DL
Tel: 01767 680551
Fax: 01767 692365
DX 47804 SANDY
www.rspb.org.uk

29/4/02

Dear Michael,

Thank you for your letter dated 25/4/02.

I am not sure what context "pigeon's milk" was mentioned on the TV programme but I found the following information on a web search.

Food for young: Both male and female parent pigeons produce a special substance called "pigeon milk," which they feed to their hatchlings during their first week of life. Pigeon milk is made in a special part of the bird's digestive system called the "crop." When hatchlings are about one week old, the parents start regurgitating seeds with crop milk; eventually seeds replace the pigeon milk.

Sleeveless Errands
The most common prank was to send someone on a 'sleeveless errand,' which meant sending them to search for a non-existent product. Young apprentices working in the shops of tradesmen were frequent victims of this trick. For instance, they might be sent to the market to search for hen's teeth, pigeon's milk, a history of Eve's grandmother, striped paint, a soft-pointed chisel, a box of straight hooks, sweet vinegar, a stick with one end, or a penny's worth of strap-oil or elbow grease. Alternatively, they might be sent to a saddler's shop to ask for some strong strapping, at which point, if they were not careful, they would receive what they asked for across their shoulders. Or they might be sent to ask for a 'long stand,' whereupon they would be told that they could stand for as long as they wished.

Yours sincerely

Ian Peters

BirdLife
INTERNATIONAL

Jenny Plackett
Assistant Director
Devon Guild of Craftsmen
Riverside Mill
Bovey Tracey
Devon TQ13 9AF

Dear Ms Plackett

I am writing to you as part of my quest for an unusual item; namely details about courses in the ancient craft of epoch-making.

Having chanced upon your guild on the Internet it occurred to me that since the Devon Guild of Craftsmen involves so many craftsmen of various backgrounds there might well be the chance of my obtaining some substantial advice about the aforementioned craft which I am so eagerly trying to study and, indeed, at which I might try my hand.

Over the years I have applied myself to the study and practice of various arts and crafts ranging from compiling framed pictures from tamed slug trails to building scale models of plague villages from pieces of dead elm wood. Sadly, my attempts have left much to be desired and I have not found the satisfaction I have sought in these areas.

It is for this reason I would like to join the ranks of some of the great names of history, such as Columbus, Drake and Genghis Khan, by learning to mould the materials of the present to influence the happenings of the future. In short I would love to become a qualified epoch-maker.

Doubtless you have many requests of this kind on a regular basis and so I thank you for your time and kind consideration and look forward to hearing from you in the very near future.

Sincerely

Michael A. Lee

The
**Devon Guild
of Craftsmen**

Riverside Mill
Bovey Tracey, Devon
TQ13 9AF

Tel: 01626 832223
Fax: 01626 834220
E-mail: devonguild@crafts.org.uk
Website: www.crafts.org.uk

Mr M A Lee
Somewhere in West Yorkshire

16th April 2002

Dear Michael Lee

Re: Courses in Epoch-making

Thank you very much for your recent letter, which my colleagues and I read with much interest.

Unfortunately we cannot recommend any particular courses to you because, as far as we know, none exist. Obviously a niche in the market, should you find such an Epoch-Maker, perhaps you could offer yourself as an apprentice and, having acquired the necessary skill and experience, run training courses for the benefit of other interested novices? Please keep us advised of your progress – part of our role as an educational charity is to provide exactly this sort of information on continuing professional development to the public.

Whilst writing, I must mention that we were particularly fascinated to read of your framed slug trail pictures – do you happen to have any images on slide of this work? It would indeed be a marvellous addition to our already comprehensive slide library.

I wish you the best of luck in the development of your work, and look forward to hearing of your progress.

Yours sincerely

**Jenny Plackett
Assistant Director**

Registered Charity No. 296568
A company limited by guarantee
No. 2026446

Head of Customer Services
Boots the Chemists
PO Box 5300
Nottingham NG90 1AA

Dear Sir/Madam

I am writing to you as part of my quest for an unusual item; namely an effective anti-wrinkle cream for the mirror in my en suite bathroom here at home in the northern town of Huddersfield.

It is fair to say that at 42 years of age there are few things that readily surprise or shock me. Over the years I have observed a wide range of phenomena in a variety of locations and situations and rarely am I taken aback at events around me. Just yesterday, however, there occurred a rather shocking exception to the rule when I looked into the bathroom mirror and noticed with a degree of horror that it had developed wrinkles. Sad to say, these wrinkles are positioned on the surface of the mirror in such a way as to correspond with various parts of my own face when I am standing in my usual position in readiness for teeth-cleaning and tie-fastening.

In this regard I would be most grateful if you could advise me with reference to the range of available anti-wrinkle creams that could remove these worrying bathroom furniture wrinkles as well as ensuring that the underlying reflecting surface is left intact and without damage. I am also in the process of writing to the Professor of Physics at Oxford University to better understand how this strange phenomenon has developed and will keep you informed if appropriate.

Many thanks indeed for your time and kind consideration and I look forward to hearing from you in the very near future.

Sincerely

M. A. Lee

Michael A. Lee

By Appointment to
Her Majesty The Queen, Chemists,
Boots The Chemists Ltd., Nottingham.

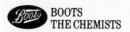
BOOTS
THE CHEMISTS

CS\1221146

Mr M A Lee
Somewhere in West Yorkshire

Customer Service
PO Box 5300
Nottingham
NG90 1AA

Tel: 08450 70 80 90
Fax: 0115 959 5525
Minicom: 08450 70 80 91
Email: btc.cshelpdesk
@boots.co.uk

30 April 2002

Dear Mr. Lee

Thank you for your letter dated 26 April. I am sorry to learn of the problem you have experienced with your en-suite bathroom mirror.

I can appreciate the distress this has caused you. Have you found this with just the one mirror or are others in your house affected?

We do have a wide selection of anti-ageing products in our stores. As this is quite an unusual problem I would suggest you call into one of our larger stores and speak to the No7 Consultant. She will be able to advise you on what products are more suitable for your requirements. Alternatively we do have selected stores which offer beauty treatments.

I personally have experienced a similar problem and now use Boots Time Delay products which I can highly recommend. The range has creams which protect, conceal and repair.

I do hope you are able to find a product to help and that you can return to normal tie-fastening and teeth-cleaning without the worrying wrinkles.

Yours sincerely

Pam Summers
Customer Manager

Boots The Chemists Ltd
Registered office
Nottingham NG2 3AA
Registered London 928555
A subsidiary of
The Boots Company PLC

**Pam Summers
Customer Manager
Boots the Chemists
PO Box 5300
Nottingham NG90 1AA**

Dear Ms Summers

First and foremost may I thank you for your swift and helpful reply to my enquiries about my wrinkle-festooned bathroom mirror. In answer to your question about other mirror involvement I am sad to say that the problem is now house-wide and all the mirrors are similarly affected. I very much appreciate your advice and will endeavour to heed your suggestions as soon as possible.

In the meantime I wonder if might ask for help in a second area of concern that is creating something of a personal challenge to me at present?

It was with great consternation that I heard my wife suggest to me recently that I ought to involve myself to a greater degree in the everyday household chores such as cooking, washing-up and ironing here in our Huddersfield home. She provided a long and eloquent summary of my existing shortfalls as far as the practicalities of domestic activity are concerned and also intimated that the solution to the present predicament would be the application of copious amounts of 'elbow grease'.

Since I am a firm believer in the principles of both constructive criticism and taking a literal view of feedback presented to me I decided that I would indeed pursue the option of applying some of the aforementioned grease to my own elbows if only I could find an appropriate brand. Doubtless you will appreciate the cold shoulder my wife will show me if I don't show her a greased elbow or two as soon as possible!

Although I have already contacted various companies that specialise in heavy-duty industrial greases that might prepare me for the certain onslaught and challenges of increased home-based duties, I would also be most interested to know if Boots the Chemists offer a brand of tailor-made elbow grease that would fit my requirements.

Many thanks indeed for your time and kind consideration and I look forward to hearing from you in the very near future.

Sincerely

M. A. Lee

Michael A. Lee

By Appointment to
Her Majesty The Queen, Chemists,
Boots The Chemists Ltd, Nottingham.

CS\1221146

Mr M A Lee
Somewhere in West Yorkshire

Customer Service
PO Box 5300
Nottingham
NG90 1AA

Tel: 08450 70 80 90
Fax: 0115 959 5525
Minicom: 08450 70 80 91
Email: btc.cshelpdesk
        @boots.co.uk

8 May 2002

Dear Mr. Lee

Thank you for your reply dated 1 May.

I have to say I thought it would spread to all the mirrors in your house. Hopefully by using the products recommended the problem will be reduced in a few weeks.

With regard to 'elbow grease,' this is something not widely asked for any more. However if you speak to a Pharmacist in store they should be able to make some up to your requirements. Alternatively our Botanics range have Intensive Moisturisers and creams which may be of help to you.

Should you find this extra work tiring we also sell a very good range of vitamin tablets which will help to build you up and give you extra energy.

I am a great believer in shared household chores and am pleased to learn that you will be getting involved.

Yours sincerely

Pam Summers
Customer Manager

Boots The Chemists Ltd
Registered office
Nottingham NG2 3AA
Registered London 928555
A subsidiary of
The Boots Company PLC

Somewhere in West Yorkshire
30 April 2002

The Director General
MI5
PO Box 3255
London SW1P 1AE

Dear Sir/Madam

I am writing to you as part of my quest for an unusual item; namely a recipe for the tastiest chicken madras in the UK.

Surfing the net a little earlier this evening, I was delighted to read through a section of MI5's official website entitled 'Myths and Misunderstandings' and subsequently felt both reassured as far as security measures are concerned as well as inspired as far as cooking is concerned. Let me explain.

I was left in no doubt by the clarity of communication within the aforementioned section that members or former members of MI5 are not at liberty to disclose without lawful authority any information, reference, security or intelligence matters to the public since this would be in breach of the Official Secrets Act. This makes eminent sense to me and I am pleased to learn that there are still, in this chaotic and confused century, vital safeguards to preserve the high and necessary standards of British intelligence and its confidential status.

I was equally pleased to read, however, that such security measures do not preclude the disclosure of information relating to the colour of the carpets at MI5 HQ, which I understand are blue – a good choice – and the fact that a rather tasty chicken madras is served at the in-house restaurant. In this regard I wonder if you might advise me regarding the amounts of coriander and chilli peppers that are included in this mouth-watering dish and I will try out the MI5 recipe in the very near future.

If this recipe finds its way into the public domain it could well be featured on the menus of Indian takeaways as dish number 007!

Many thanks indeed for your time and kind consideration and I look forward to hearing from you in the near future.

Sincerely

Michael A. Lee

REGNUM · DEFENDE

PO BOX 3255
LONDON
SW1P 1AE

Mr M A Lee   30 May 2002
Somewhere in West Yorkshire

Dear Mr Lee

Thank you for your letter of 30 April. I apologise for the delay in replying.

Our catering department use a commercially available madras paste as a basis for the Chicken
Madras served in our restaurant.

Yours sincerely,

The Director General

Somewhere in West Yorkshire
29 April 2002

**Head of Customer Services
Nestlé UK Ltd
York YO91 1XY**

Dear Sir/Madam

I am writing to you as part of my quest for an unusual item; namely a chocolate fireguard.

Involved as I am in industry and specifically in the complex world of sales and marketing, I work with a large number of individuals whose range of skills, attitudes and indeed performance achievements are amazingly varied.

Doubtless you would agree that it is a straightforward task to choose rewards of a tangible and motivational kind for those whose abilities and achievements are noteworthy and require explicit recognition of a material nature.

However, it proves an endless and far more difficult task to provide gifts that involve a message of stark and obvious meaning to those whose successes could be best summarised on the back of a postage stamp and who require a hint of sarcastic encouragement before finding that the regional manager is standing next to them in battle fatigues with a P45. It is for this reason that I write to you.

If you could supply me with a number of modestly priced chocolate fireguards, certain of my colleagues could receive a symbolic item providing integral feedback in the sweetest way I can currently conceive.

There would certainly not be a bitter taste left in their mouths and perhaps the significant uptake of energy-providing glucose would provide the impetus for action and future industry.

Many thanks for your time and consideration and I look forward to hearing from you in the near future.

Sincerely

M. A. Lee

Michael A. Lee

P.S. All this word-processing has given me an appetite. Feel free to send samples of your more conventional chocolate creations if appropriate. I have two small children and very little money!

Nestlé UK Ltd

YORK YO91 1XY

TELEPHONE (01904) 604604
FACSIMILE (01904) 604534

www.nestle.co.uk

Mr M A Lee
Somewhere in West Yorkshire

DIRECT LINE: 0800 000030

0888216A   **3 May 2002** DIRECT FAX: (01904) 603461

YOUR REF.   OUR REF.   DATE

Dear Michael

Thank you for your recent amusing letter.

We are sorry to hear that you are having trouble motivating your Sales Force.

We are sorry to inform you that Chocolate Fireguards have been withdrawn from our range due to the vast amount of them being returned due to heat damage.

We hope that this is not too disappointing a reply, however we have included some goodies for your children. Thank you once again for taking the trouble to contact us and good luck in your task .

Yours sincerely

Joanne Nudd
Call Centre Supervisor
Consumer Services

**The Archbishop of York
Bishopthorpe Palace
Bishopthorpe
York
North Yorkshire YO23 2GE**

Dear Sir

I am writing to you as part of my quest for an unusual item; namely the title 'Son of a Gun' within the Church of England.

As a 42-year-old Yorkshire man, I have, over the course of many years, watched with great interest a vast selection of Westerns both on TV and in the cinema, and have even read a number of paperbacks of a cowboy nature. When reviewing these films and books it is rather staggering to note how often a character appears who is known as the 'Son of a Gun' and who, in many cases, provides the viewer or reader with a figure of moral fortitude and example in comparison to the pistol-toting father who rode the Wild West before him.

As an upright and honest individual who believes in the law and order of contemporary society, the importance of family life and of open and honest government based on Judaeo-Christian traditions, I would myself like to be considered a 21st-century 'Son of a Gun' in the England of today and specifically within the structure of the Church. I could then be seen as a modern-day 'Anglican Shane' travelling from place to place representing all things bright and beautiful and embodying the principles of strength and peace.

My greatest difficulty in claiming a right to the title is the fact that my blood lineage does not actually involve a father who possessed or made use of any form of gun. (All he owned in the potential weapons department was a small penknife!) Consequently I wondered if, in order to provide a *bona-fide* basis for my application for the aforementioned title, I might be adopted, at least in a symbolic manner, by a canon! I would then truly be the 'Son of a Gun' and could wear my robes and stetson with pride and dignity.

Many thanks for your time and consideration. I look forward to hearing from you in the very near future regarding how to take this application forward to the next stage.

Sincerely

M. A. Lee

Michael A. Lee

THE BISHOP OF WAKEFIELD - *The Right Reverend Nigel McCulloch*

Bishop's Lodge   Woodthorpe Lane   Wakefield   West Yorkshire   WF2 6JL
Tel: 01924-255349   Fax: 01924-250202   E-mail:bishop@wakefield.anglican.org

09 May 2002

Mr M A Lee
Somewhere in West Yorkshire

Dear Mr. Lee,

Thank you for your interesting letter concerning your desire to serve as a modern day 'Church of England Shane' and to obtain a bona fide basis for your claim to the title 'Son of a Gun'.

However, your request poses real problems as Wakefield is an 'equal opportunities' diocese. If I were to grant such a request, it might well open the floodgates to many other applicants for the said title. Some of these may be women and that would necessitate the creation of a precedent, as we would be forced to create the title 'Daughter of a Gun'. In fact the whole project may be perceived as politically incorrect. Perhaps the best compromise would be the title 'Offspring of a Gun'.

There again we run into the murky waters of political incorrectness. Referring to a person by their job title, ethnic origin or medical condition is now unacceptable. To be the son of a 'Gun' would not be permissible. The 'Son of a person who has/had, owns/owned, uses/used a Gun' would be more acceptable.

Your suggestion of adoption by a Canon, symbolic or otherwise, also poses problems. As defined in the 'Concise Oxford Dictionary', a Canon is a 'member of a cathedral chapter', but the weapon of war to which I believe you meant to allude is defined by that publication as 'Cannon: a large, heavy gun'. Over the former I have a certain amount of influence, but over the latter, regrettably none. Therefore I find myself unable to accede to your request.

/I

I believe that the term 'Gunner' is still in current use by Her Majesty's armed forces. It may be that a request made to the appropriate department of that authority might meet with more success.

May I wish you every success in your quest to become an 'Offspring of a Gun (Gunner)' that it might enable you to wear your Stetson with pride. I too, as a boy, enjoyed games of Cowboys and Native Americans.

Yours sincerely

Nigel Wakeford

Bishopthorpe Palace
Bishopthorpe
York
YO23 2GE

Tel: (01904) 707021
Fax: (01904) 709204
E-mail: office@bishopthorpe.u-net.com
www.bishopthorpepalace.co.uk

The Venerable Alan Dean
Special Adviser to the Archbishop

01 May 2002

Dear Mr Lee,

I write in acknowledgement of your letter to the Archbishop, dated 29th April 2002 - but whose contents cannot but lead one to suppose that it might have been more appropriately dated 1st April 2002.

Be that as it may, I have to tell you that - with or without the adoptive lineage of which you speak - the formal appointment which you have in mind simply does not lie within the Archbishop's gift.

Accordingly, any representational role in the matter of 'all things bright and beautiful'(etc.) would have to be undertaken solo: that is, without commissioning or benefit of letters patent.

With all good wishes - and with thanks for brightening our day!

Yours very sincerely

Mr M A Lee
Somewhere in West Yorkshire

The Venerable Alan Dean
Special Advisor to the Archbishop
Bishopthorpe Palace
Bishopthorpe
York YO23 2GE

Dear Sir

First and foremost may I thank you for your letter dated 1 May 2002 in reply to my enquiries about becoming a 'Son of a Gun' within the Church of England.

I was disappointed to hear that the appointment of such a person does not lie within the Archbishop's gift but am nevertheless appreciative of your response as it has allowed me to consider alternative opportunities for my attention and midlife aspirations.

In this regard I am writing to you once again as part of my quest for an unusual item; namely the title 'Spire Straightener' in relation to the age-old problem regarding the crooked spire of Chesterfield's ancient church. I presume this falls within the geographical area managed by the Archbishop of York. Let me explain.

Fascinated by myths and legends, I recently focused on a website while surfing the net. This related the well-known theory that the famous crooked spire of St Mary's was caused by the uncontrolled rage of the Devil as he fled, cloven foot pierced by a hoofing nail, from the Blacksmith of Bollsover, damaging the spire en route. Call me a cynic if you will, but this I find hard to believe as historical fact!

In stark contrast, however, I do think that the alternative explanation – that the twisting was the result of the spire leaning in an attempt to watch in astonishment as a virgin was joined to her husband in the wonderful union of matrimony – is highly plausible. I also happen to believe that it is eminently likely that the spire will straighten itself if another virgin marries in the church at a later date.

This is where I may be able to help. My wife, who is, incidentally, a midwife, mentioned to me in a rather discrete fashion that one of her colleagues, a shy and somewhat introverted lady in her late 40s, has neither enjoyed the pleasures of a stable marriage nor indeed those of an unstable marriage, common-law relationship or even a passionate moment through the eyes of indiscretion or the base of an empty wine glass. Strange as it sounds in these modern times, this spinster is nothing less than a virgin!

It occurred to me that should you know of any bachelors of the Chesterfield parish who have, to date, struggled with the challenges of relationship and are willing to meet with this lady we might, between us, have a plan for free spire restoration. If you were to choose a bachelor who is happy to forego pre-nuptual activity of any physical kind and enjoy a wedding ceremony with the chaste lady to whom I have already referred, the spire will, as tradition states, return to its original non-crooked state. A cunning plan, I am sure you will agree!

. . . continued

I am not at all interested in seeking monetary reward for such information but would get my satisfaction from seeing two lonely hearts gain comfort and companionship and also by receiving the official title, 'Spire Straightener', an accolade that will doubtless serve my future reputation and career path well.

Doubtless you receive many letters of this kind on a regular basis and so I thank you for your time and kind consideration and I look forward to hearing from you in the very near future.

Sincerely

Michael A. Lee

THE OFFICE OF
THE ARCHBISHOP OF YORK

Bishopthorpe Palace
Bishopthorpe
York
YO23 2GE

Tel: (01904) 707021
Fax: (01904) 709204
E-mail: office@bishopthorpe.u-net.com
www.bishopthorpepalace.co.uk

The Venerable Alan Dean
Special Adviser to the Archbishop

23 May 2002

Dear Mr Lee,

How good it was to hear from you again - and that so soon!

However, I fear that, once again, your plan falls at the first hurdle. The fact is that the affections of the good people of Chesterfield are so very firmly wedded to their church's twisted spire that the mere thought of its being straightened would be entirely anathema to them.   In short, there is simply no call for a 'spire straightener'.

Disappointing though this may be to you, I have every confidence that you will be able to put the bravest of faces upon your chagrin and resume your search for that elusive 'something' which beckons to you from beyond the shores of that more pedestrian reality which detains the rest of us.

Doubtless you will give us news of progress - and, needless to say, we ourselves are a-tiptoe in fascinated anticipation!

With all good wishes
yours sincerely

Mr M A Lee
Somewhere in West Yorkshire

The Venerable Alan Dean
Special Advisor to the Archbishop
Bishopthorpe Palace
Bishopthorpe
York YO23 2GE

Dear Sir

Once again, may I take this opportunity to thank you for taking the time and effort to respond to my recently suggested plan to untwist the spire of Chesterfield Parish Church.

I was a little disappointed that the plan will remain a concept without application and, indeed, disappointed for my wife's friend whose future appears to be one of bleak though committed spinsterhood but I do appreciate your comments and explanation regarding safeguarding the continuity of 'things familiar' for Chesterfield's community. I will, as you quite rightly suggest, move forward in my quest for the unusual and focus on activities other than spire straightening.

In this respect I wonder if you may be able to help me in my desire to acquire the position of 'Officially Recognised Parish Worm Charmer' in the wonderful parish of Fatfield in County Durham, famed, of course, for the fabled Lambton Worm of times past.

I did write to the Bishop of Durham in reference to this matter several months ago. Sadly, I failed to receive a reply and concluded that the appointment of such a key position might well lie more within the remit of the Archbishop.

Having recently read on an Internet website the story of the Lambton Worm, it occurred to me that had the original worm been female and cast into the fabled well by Sir John Lambton while pregnant, there is a jolly good chance that other monstrous worms of gargantuan proportions may well have been born before the slaying of the mother and have been living undetected beneath the ground for several centuries and perhaps in large numbers.

It is not beyond the bounds of possibility that one of these days another large, milk-stealing, baby-eating worm might emerge from its subterranean burrow or well corner and create mayhem among the community within the Fatfield parish.

This could have catastrophic consequences for church attendance on Sunday mornings and indeed at evensong though it may well keep the grave diggers rather busy. Herein lies a potential job opportunity for me and hence the reason for my writing this application to your good self! In a similar manner to the Indian snake charmer, I have developed an intriguing mastery of hypnotising worms by playing an Irish penny whistle. Within seconds of my playing a ballad these slithering beats of the ground become transfixed and hence are ready for capture or despatch.

As a longstanding member of the Fell Runners Association I am reasonably quick on my feet and can move around the worm with a fleetness of foot a little reminiscent of Mohammed Ali in his earlier days.

. . . continued

I am rather nimble with a sword and I have no particular sympathy for worms other than those normal-sized creatures that live in my compost heap and herbaceous borders and carry out the marvellous task of breaking down and aerating my soil. I would therefore have no difficulty in trapping or slaying the monstrous offspring of the original legend should the occasion arise and indeed would feel such a deed fully justified if community safety was threatened.

Doubtless you receive many enquiries of this kind as I appreciate the market for employment is rather competitive these days and so thank you for your time and kind consideration. Please rest assured, however, that candidates with skills and abilities such as mine are few and far between.

I look forward to hearing from you in the very near future and in anticipation of receiving an invitation for interview can assure you that I will continue my regular rehearsal of the penny whistle and fine tuning my swordsmanship.

Sincerely

Michael A. Lee

THE OFFICE OF
THE ARCHBISHOP OF YORK

Bishopthorpe Palace
Bishopthorpe
York
YO23 2GE

Tel: (01904) 707021
Fax: (01904) 709204
E-mail: office@bishopthorpe.u-net.com
www.bishopthorpepalace.co.uk

The Venerable Alan Dean
Special Adviser to the Archbishop

26 June 2002

Dear Mr Lee,

My grateful thanks for your latest offering of 26th May 2002.

It was heartening to learn of your continued readiness to offer your services in ways which are, to say the least, imaginative.

However, whilst I am filled with admiration for your facility upon the (Irish) penny whistle and whilst your physical agility and swordsmanship (would it be foil, epee or sabre?) leave me trembling and breathless, I remain concerned that once again you seem intent on seeking to deploy your skills to combat problems in areas where no discernible problem exists.

Could it simply be that you are exhibiting an extraordinary degree of prescience ? - or could it be something rather more disquieting?   We shall, as they say, continue to watch this space.

Yours very sincerely

Mr M A Lee
Somewhere in West Yorkshire

Somewhere in West Yorkshire
2 May 2002

The Vicar
Chesterfield Parish Church
Derbyshire

Dear Sir

I am writing to you as part of my quest for an unusual item; namely the title 'Spire Restoration Manager' with relation to the age-old problem regarding the crooked spire of your ancient church. Let me explain.

Fascinated by myths and legends, I recently found a website relating the well-known theory that the famous crooked spire of St Mary's was caused by the uncontrolled rage of the Devil as he fled, cloven foot pierced by a hoofing nail, from the Blacksmith of Bollsover, damaging the spire en route. Call me a cynic if you will, but this I find hard to believe as historical fact! In stark contrast, however, I do think that the alternative explanation is highly plausible: that the twisting was the result of the spire leaning over in an attempt to watch in astonishment as a virgin was joined to her husband in the wonderful union of matrimony. I also believe that it is eminently likely the spire will straighten itself if another virgin marries in the church at a later date. Surely this is within the realm of credibility!

This is where I may be able to help. My wife, who is, incidentally, a midwife, discretely mentioned to me that one of her colleagues, a shy and somewhat introverted lady in her late 40s, has neither enjoyed the pleasures of a stable marriage nor indeed those of an unstable marriage, common-law relationship or even a passionate moment through the eyes of indiscretion or an empty wine glass. Strange as it sounds, this aforementioned spinster is nothing less than a virgin! I am not, at this point in time, willing to divulge her name.

It occurred to me that should you know of any bachelors of the parish who are willing to meet with this lady we might, between us, have a plan for free spire restoration. If you were to choose a bachelor who is happy to forego pre-nuptual activity of any physical kind and enjoy a wedding ceremony with the chaste lady to whom I have already referred, the spire will, as tradition states, return to its original non-crooked state and not one single penny will need to be paid to surveyors, tradesmen or builders' labourers for the work involved. A cunning plan, I am sure you will agree!

I am not at all interested in seeking monetary reward for such information but would get my satisfaction from seeing two lonely hearts gain comfort and companionship in their togetherness, and also by receiving the official title, 'Spire Restoration Manager' which would be a wonderful addition to my rather brief and uninteresting C.V.

Doubtless you receive many letters of this kind on a regular basis and so I thank you for your time and kind consideration and I look forward to hearing from you in the very near future.

Sincerely

M. A. Lee

Michael A. Lee

P.S. Failing this, I also undertake basic gardening duties and can dig graves by the bucketful provided there is not too much pebble-strewn boulder clay in the area.

Chesterfield
Parish Church

Parish Office   01246 206506
Vicarage   01246 232937

28 CROMWELL ROAD
CHESTERFIELD
S40 4TH

Mr M A Lee
Somewhere in West Yorkshire

19 June, 2002

Dear Mr Lee,

Thank you for your letter, and your novel answer to our architectural oddity. I am sorry it has taken a while to reply but I have been busy identifying suitable candidates for your lady friend's hand. I have now managed to find three suitable bachelors of mature years who might fulfil the role you had in mind, which at least allows her a degree of choice.

However, I perceive a difficulty. As you will know, the marriage ceremony must be public but the marriage itself is not effected simply by the ceremony in church, but must also be consummated. My three candidates are willing, even enthusiastic so to do, granted the frustrating purity of their lives hitherto. The problem arises because the people of Chesterfield have an emotional – and indeed an economic –attachment to the spire of such intensity that anyone who managed to straighten it might well be strung up from the nearest lamppost. My friends are feeling their necks, rather anxiously.

How may I put this with appropriate delicacy? They are asking me what guarantees are on offer to ensure that the pleasure of the marriage bed will be sufficient to offset any dire consequences? A man may be willing to die for love – but for an uncertain one night stand?

Yours sincerely,

Richard Knight

PS My gardener is a total disaster, and any help would be gratefully received.

The Duke & Duchess of Devonshire
Chatsworth House
Matlock
Derbyshire

Dear Sir & Madam

I am writing to you as part of my quest for an unusual item; namely a permit to pan for gold in the four large reservoir lakes, the Emperor Fountain, the Cascades and the river belonging to your wonderful Chatsworth House estate.

Rather than accompany members of a recognised gold-panning or prospecting club to the aforementioned areas of potential water-borne fortune, I would much prefer to undertake my own gold-panning enterprise as a solo venture and play the part of a modern-day Klondike prospector both for relaxation and perhaps to make the lucky discovery of an obscenely large gold nugget. I would even be happy to bring along my own Thermos flask!

I can assure you that my gold-panning activities would not interfere with any of the other concerns undertaken in, on or around Chatsworth and I will be careful not to leave any trace of my endeavours. I have no mule to disgrace itself and am myself a clean and fastidious person.

Should I be fortunate enough to find that most precious of minerals in the area I can assure you that I will keep such a discovery to ourselves and thus avoid any consequent gold rush that would doubtless be detrimental to the integrity of the countryside and surrounding flora and fauna. Would a 50/50 share of the findings be agreeable to yourselves?

As a Yorkshire man with a pioneering spirit and desire to become a self-made millionaire, I would be most interested in any help and advice you can provide.

I thank you for your time and consideration and look forward to hearing from you in the very near future.

Sincerely

Michael A. Lee

The Trustees of the Chatsworth Settlement

Estate Office Derbyshire Estates

Edensor Bakewell Derbyshire DE45 1PJ
Tel: Baslow (01246) 565300
Fax: Baslow (01246) 583464

Agent: R. B. Wardle F.R.I.C.S.
Deputy Agent: N. J. W. Wood A.R.I.C.S.

13 May 2002

RBW/vmb/024

Mr M A Lee
Somewhere in West Yorkshire

Dear Mr Lee

Gold-panning on Chatsworth Estate

I refer to your letter of the 30th April addressed to the Duke and Duchess of Devonshire who have asked me to reply on their behalf.

I am afraid I am going to disappoint you by saying it will not be possible to give you permission to pan for gold at Chatsworth. As you might imagine, we get a considerable number of requests from people wishing to search for treasure of one sort or another and it has therefore been necessary for us to adopt a policy of dealing only with one recognised group. If we were to accede to individual requests, it would be unfair to all those who have been turned down in the past and so it simply remains for me to wish you good luck with your pioneering spirit and desire to become a self-made millionaire.

Yours sincerely

R B Wardle
Agent

Somewhere in West Yorkshire
1 May 2002

Marketing Manager
Ready Brek Brand
Weetabix Ltd
Burton Latimer
Kettering
Northants NN15 5JR

Dear Sir/Madam

I am writing to you as part of my quest for an unusual item; namely the variety of Ready Brek cereal advertised on TV a few years ago that helps children to glow in the dark.

Now aged 42, I remember well the memorable advertising for your most excellent breakfast cereal, demonstrating the way small children who ate Ready Brek on a regular basis were provided with a bright and distinct aura around their bodies and were protected from the chill winds of winter. I presume that the film of these luminous children was taken before the introduction of special effects and the impact of such viewing has certainly had a significant and long-lasting effect on me.

A few weeks ago I bought a 750mg box of Original Ready Brek for the first time in many years and served a generous portion of this tasty breakfast food to my three-year-old son George. Possessing a voracious appetite, he ate the contents of his bowl with enthusiastic haste and soon afterwards showed all the signs of restored energy levels and an associated degree of boisterousness in his play. However, sad to say, he did not glow even in the very remotest sense of the word.

Over the next week or two I increased the amount of Ready Brek for George's breakfast by an additional bowl a day. At the end of this period and several boxes of Ready Brek later he was consuming the equivalent of ten bowls of cereal each morning. Although the side effects – which included severe bloating and abdominal distension, intractable wind and a tendency to lie still for long periods of time – were a little disturbing, I persevered with the regime hoping for luminescence. Alas, not a single shaft of light was to be seen anywhere.

I came to the conclusion that perhaps today's Ready Brek is a modified version of the brand I saw advertised so often many years ago. I wondered if I might be able to purchase the original 'Original' cereal, if indeed you are still able to manufacture and supply this.

You will be pleased to know that since I cut back George's rations to just one bowl of cereal a day, along with a piece of buttered toast, he has recovered from his overfeeding and has begun to smile again. He still doesn't glow in the dark but, since the lighter spring mornings have arrived, he doesn't need to. When autumn arrives, of course, the same challenges will doubtless arise.

Many thanks for your time and kind consideration in this matter and I look forward to hearing from you with appropriate advice in the very near future.

Sincerely

M. A. Lee

Michael A. Lee

248-46-5/ajl/V1.50

Mr M A Lee
Somewhere in West Yorkshire

May 9, 2002

Dear Mr Lee

Many thanks for your letter of May 1, though we were sorry to hear how disappointed you were that your son did not 'glow', even after such a large helping of Ready Brek.

Please tell George not to worry. Times have changed and with the success of that memorable campaign, we no longer feel it necessary to make, what now appears, such an obvious statement. Those who need to know have the knowledge and appreciation of how healthful and satisfying a bowl of Ready Brek can be. And those who, for whatever reason, do not know, well what more can I say?!

For old times sake, you can see the 1980s advert in the Time Machine section of our new Internet site. We hope you will be able to visit www.weetabix.co.uk very soon.

In the meantime, we trust you and young George will continue to enjoy the great taste of Ready Brek

Yours sincerely

Paul Blomley

Paul Blomley
Consumer Services Officer
e-mail: consumerservice@weetabix.co.uk

Weetabix Ltd.

THE LEADING BRITISH BREAKFAST CEREAL MANUFACTURER
Weetabix Limited, Burton Latimer, Kettering, NN15 5JR

Head of Customer Care
Warburtons Ltd
Hereford House
Hereford Street
Bolton BL1 8JB

Dear Sir/Madam

I am writing to you as part of my quest for an unusual item; namely a sliced loaf whose slices, when buttered, are guaranteed to fall butter side up. In this regard I could think of no better organisation to which I could direct my initial enquiries than your good selves at Warburtons.

Doubtless there are innumerable people across the UK who stand in amazement at the scientific and technological achievements of Western man in the 21st century. Each day the newspapers contain information about the very latest developments in space exploration and exciting medical breakthroughs, super-computers and even robotics.

The children of the early Warburton family several years ago would be amazed to see the world in which we now live, with its complexity of microwave ovens, widescreen TVs, interactive laptop gadgets that can recognise and respond to human voices, and even cloned sheep.

Perhaps in the light of contemporary automation, they would regret so much time spent in days gone by kneading dough by hand! Yet, despite all the time, effort and energy that has been invested over the years to create this hi-tech society and the opulence and convenience that this permits, I have yet to find a solution to an age-old problem: how to avoid the buttered side of my sliced bread or toast from landing face down on a dusty linoleum surface or hairy carpet smeared with my children's cast-off bananas. I am significantly stressed at the very thought of this regular occurrence repeating itself once again.

Many thanks indeed for your time and kind consideration in this matter and I would be most grateful for any help and advice you can offer.

Sincerely

M. A. Lee

Michael A. Lee

ODE TO A LOAF

What a pity, what a shame
Your plight we feel is clearly plain

Much to our regret we have to say
Its our bet it's just the way

It's sods law or so they say
That buttered bread falls that way

We would suggest you keep tight hold
Once buttered our bread becomes quite bold

There is no more that we can say
"Respect the Bread", it's the best way.

Anon. Circa 2002

Warburtons Limited
Hereford House
Hereford Street
Bolton BL1 8JB

Telephone 01204 556600
Facsimile 01204 532283
www.warburtons.co.uk

Registered Office
Back o'th' Bank House
Hereford Street
Bolton BL1 8HJ

Registered in England
No. 178711

INVESTOR IN PEOPLE

Somewhere in West Yorkshire
4 May 2002

Head of Lost Property
Transport for London
Transport Trading Limited
Lost Property Office
200 Baker Street
London NW1 5RZ

Dear Sir/Madam

I am writing to you as part of my quest for an unusual item; namely my lost 'umph' which I may well have mislaid somewhere within the London Underground network a few weeks ago.

Aged 42, I have spent the best part of 30 years enjoying the spare-time activity of cross-country and fell running. For many years I enjoyed a position in various races in the top 50th percentile and could run with fleetness of foot without any significant effort of lung or muscle. Although a little tired the day after a race or long training run, I would nevertheless recover quickly and be as fresh as the proverbial daisy for the next event in no time at all. The same was true of my daily working life. I would begin in the morning with energy levels of the highest, work with all cylinders firing and still have the time, inclination and wherewithal to party late into the night at the end of a busy and productive day. In short I had lots of 'umph'.

Sadly, I have to inform you that much of my 'umph' has disappeared. My 'get up and go' has regrettably 'got up and gone'! I now run more slowly with far more effort required and my recovery time has increased considerably, to the point where legs and lungs still show the signs of stiffness and stretch several days after a bout of training or a short fell-race. I wake up for work feeling tired, fulfil my daily obligations with a sense of fatigue, and retire to my bed in an exhausted and worn-out fashion.

In this regard I have searched high and low for my lost 'umph' but cannot find it anywhere and I have begun to wonder if I lost it when travelling on the Underground earlier this year. If it has turned up in your lost-property office I would be grateful to have it back again!

Many thanks for your time and kind consideration in this matter and I look forward to hearing from you in the very near future.

Sincerely and anxiously

Michael A. Lee

Transport *for* **London**

Transport Trading Limited

Lost Property

Mr M A Lee
Somewhere in West Yorkshire

17 May 2002

Dear Mr Lee

Thank you for your letter of the 5 May 2002.

It must have come as quite a shock
To find that time had slowed your clock

To notice that your 'umph' had gone astray
You must have realised there had to come that day

A day that your 'umph' just ran out
A day that you no longer sprint about

A day when things get lost and start falling out
Because many people come in here and shout

I've lost my hair my teeth as well
Like some of us here, so let me tell

If I had found your 'umph' I'd have spread it around
But unfortunately it was never found

Yours sincerely

Maureen Beaumont

Transport Trading Limited, Lost Property Office, 200 Baker Street, London NW1 5RZ

Registered office: Windsor House, 42-50 Victoria Street, London SW1H 0TL, Registered in England and Wales, Company Number 391 4810, VAT Number 756 2770 08

Head of Customer Service
Met Office
London Road
Bracknell
Berkshire RG12 2SZ

Dear Sir/Madam

I am writing to you as part of my quest for an unusual item; namely a silver lining from a used cloud.

Despite the passage of over 20 years since I graduated in Geography, I clearly remember one of my college lecturers explaining that once a cloud has shed its moisture in the form of rain, sleet, hailstone or snow there will, ultimately, be no cloud left as it is the very moisture that forms most of its integral structure. He did, however, fail to mention a very important if not vital piece of information; specifically, what actually happens to the silver lining once the bulk of the cloud had vanished.

Having thought long and hard about this puzzle, I initially came to the conclusion that the majority of silver cloud linings are so thin and lacking in depth that they break apart into countless minute fragments as they fall from great heights to earth and are lost among the soil, vegetation and water on the earth's surface.

However, analysing this concept a little more closely, I began to wonder if this were true also of low cloud since, as the silver lining has less far to fall, there is less chance of fragmentation and disintegration and the consequential possibility of complete sections of silver lining surviving for the picking.

It is in this regard that I write. I am not a wealthy man by any stretch of the imagination and would love nothing better than to find either a complete silver lining or indeed part of a silver lining of any recognised cloud type. I would be most grateful, therefore, if you could advise me of any locations within the UK where the chances of realising my lofty dream could be accomplished more readily. This would make me a very happy man indeed.

I realise that you must deal with many enquiries of this type on a regular basis and so I thank you for your time and kind consideration and look forward to hearing from you in the very near future.

Sincerely

Michael A. Lee

Customer Centre
PD9 Powell Duffryn House
London Road
Bracknell
RG12 2SX
Tel: 0845 3000300
Fax: 0845 3001300
e-mail: customercentre@metoffice.com

May 22, 2002

Dear Mr Lee,

Thank you for taking the time to write to the Met Office. Unfortunately we cannot advise you as to purchasing or finding a silver lining.

The proverb "Every cloud has a silver lining" has been widely used to mean *"Every difficult or depressing circumstance has its hidden consolations. There is always a reason for hope in the most desperate situations"*.

It has been used in 1915 by the First World War troops in war time song "Keep The Home Fires Burning" in Charles Dickens' "The Bleak House" written in 1852 to a quote by Radio 4 in 1994.

If you would like any further information about Meteorological events please don't hesitate to contact us.

Yours Sincerely,

Andy Marriott
Customer Centre Duty Manager

INVESTOR IN PEOPLE

The New Mayor
The Town Hall
Hartlepool

Dear Sir/Madam

I am writing to you as part of my quest for an unusual item; namely the position of 'Monkey Hanging Executive' within the Hartlepool community should this role become available in the near future. As the new and creative Mayor, I thought it best to seek your advice about securing this position since neither your predecessor nor your MP were inclined to consider me when I wrote to them at an earlier date.

Although currently living in Huddersfield, West Yorkshire, I remember as a child hearing on many occasions the tale of the hanging of the infamous 'French spy' from my dear Grandmother of the once flourishing Eden Street in West Hartlepool.

As a consequence I have wondered for many years if indeed the simian creature that suffered his or her demise from the end of a north-eastern rope had actually been craftily trained by the Napoleonic enemy and if perhaps the hanging was therefore a justified act of anti-terrorism. It is my opinion that an invasion from the Continent may well have been averted by this timely execution and that releasing this enigmatic French agent could have led to events of catastrophic significance, changing the very history of the British Isles. It is possible that, had the hanging not occurred, we might even now be suffering under a despotic Norman presidency rather than living in a democratic British society with a caring Royal Family, as we do.

Aged 41, I am most concerned at the many contemporary occasions when the French look northward with a Norman nose for trouble, complaining about our various industries and institutions and criticising our British way of life. I wonder if at some point in the near future they might once again try a dastardly trick of subterfuge and repeat their insertion of a spy, as they did so long ago.

Should this possibility become a reality, the local Hartlepool community would doubtless require the services of a competent monkey hangman and I would suggest that I am an ideal candidate for the job. Should the spy need arresting in coastal waters I am a good swimmer with a strong and determined grip. I am also a seasoned fell-runner and, being fast on my feet, believe I could outrun a monkey over distance should there be a need to catch a desperate escapee. I can jump quite a height and even climb trees! I have also had experience of scouting and am so adept at tying knots and nooses that I was once awarded a knot-tying badge.

Having spent much of my youth in the Hartlepool area, I would be quite happy to relocate. Of course, I have a good grasp of local geography, which is always of benefit if any form of hunting or tracking is involved.

I thank you for your time and consideration and look forward to hearing form you with regards to this matter in the very near future.

Yours sincerely

Michael A. Lee

STUART DRUMMOND
Mayor of Hartlepool

Our Ref:　　　SFD/DB

Your Ref:

Civic Centre
Hartlepool TS24 8AY

Tel:　　01429 266522
Fax:　　01429 523701
DX:　　60669 Hartlepool-1

HARTLEPOOL
BOROUGH COUNCIL

16th May 2002

Mr M A Lee
Somewhere in West Yorkshire

Dear Mr. Lee

Thank you for your letter dated 8th May 2002.

If the position of 'Monkey Hanging Executive' ever becomes available in Hartlepool, I will keep you in mind.

Yours sincerely

STUART DRUMMOND
Mayor

Somewhere in West Yorkshire
10 May 2002

Head of Enquiries
National Maritime Museum
Romney Road
Greenwich
London SE10 9NF

Dear Sir/Madam

I am writing to you as part of my quest for an unusual item; namely some space at the National Maritime Museum that would lend itself perfectly to my present condition, which is most accurately described as a 'complete wreck'.

Aged 42, I am a rather craggy, weather-beaten individual whose hold has been filled to capacity one too many times, causing significant leaning and the beginnings of a sinking process. It has surprised and indeed concerned me in recent months to experience an increasing stiffness in my muscles and joints early in the morning and greater weariness earlier in the evening than used to be the case; in seafaring terms my timbers are beginning to rot even though the mast is, at least for the time-being, still upright.

The waves that were visible on the top of my head a few years ago have permanently retreated and instead there is but a bare, sandy beach that provides a home only for sunburned tissue and settling dust. In short, I could be likened to a ship on the rocks and am probably good for very little but as an example of a complete human wreck.

It is on the basis of the aforementioned state of deterioration that I write to you for help. Please could you find a section of the museum where I might be seen by members of the public both as an interesting and unusual seaside exhibit as well as a stark warning of what can happen when a landlubber forgets to wash his decks, varnish the hull and replaces his lime allocation with far too much rum?

Many thanks indeed for your time and consideration and I look forward to hearing from you in the very near future.

Sincerely

Michael A. Lee

...illustrating the importance of the sea, ships, time and the stars...

Mr M A Lee
Somewhere in West Yorkshire

16th May 2002

Dear Mr Lee

Thank you for your message in a bottle dated 10th May 2002.

I am so sorry to hear about your present rather distressed state, but at least we may take comfort in the fact that you have sailed the high seas and must have many a yarn to while away the hours.

I am very sympathetic having been holed below the waterline myself only recently, although in my case it did allow for a full refit and I am now back with the fleet.

Should you be interested in any employment opportunity with us which may allow similar treatment in your case, please forward your latest curriculum vitae for our consideration. In the meantime, try to maintain a leeward station so as not to spill the rum.

Yours sincerely

A. N. Bodle

Andy Bodle
HR Director

Patron: HRH The Duke of Edinburgh, KG, KT
National Maritime Museum, Greenwich, London SE10 9NF
Tel: 020 8858 4422 Fax: 020 8312 6632 www.nmm.ac.uk

INVESTOR IN PEOPLE

Maritime GREENWICH
A WORLD HERITAGE SITE

Lord Harewood
Harewood House
Harewood
Leeds
West Yorkshire

Dear Sir

I am writing to you as part of my quest for an unusual thing; namely permission to remodel a specific part of the statue of Orpheus crafted by Astrid Zydower that stands outside your magnificent house in the midst of the formal terrace garden.

Just last week my wife and I visited Harewood House so that our two small children could meet Noddy and his friends who were visiting for the weekend, and also to see your impressive gardens and wonderful collection of birds. The day was most enjoyable with the exception of one 'not so small' detail. Let me explain.

As my family and I walked through the terraced gardens, the eyes of my wife and I fell upon the heroic figure of naked Orpheus supporting the big cat upon his muscular shoulders and standing without shame in a pose both classical and boastful. We were both shocked at the size of his sculpted inheritance but, whereas my own shock turned quickly into jealousy, my wife's became an annoying combination of glassy-eyed admiration and complete distraction. Over a week has passed and she still looks into space and frequently sighs in a most distressing manner, oblivious of my presence or obvious annoyance.

Doubtless there are scores of male visitors who share my experience of envy and utter disbelief in the dimensions of Orpheus' tail-end Charlie, and I am sure that there must be an equal number of besotted women whose beguilement following their visual encounter hinders their progress in everyday life. Perhaps you would consider my suggestion that I once again visit Harewood House, this time with hammer, chisel and sandpaper and remodel the offending member of Orpheus so all families can return home in as content a manner as possible and learn to live life with modest expectations intact.

Doubtless you would agree that my act of mercy can lead to nothing but good and perhaps, as well as helping to maintain an element of contentment for the many married and courting couples that chance upon a single sight of Orpheus, it may also help Lady Harewood and your good self in whatever emotional difficulties regular sightings of 'The Big Fellow' may have caused.

Many thanks for your time and kind consideration and I look forward to hearing from you in the very near future.

Sincerely

Michael A. Lee

P.S. I am now going out to my garage where I keep my chisel sharpener!

Leeds
LS17 9LG

14th May 2002

Mr M A Lee
Somewhere in West Yorkshire

Dear Mr Lee

Thank you for your letter raising a most important point, to wit the not inconsiderable endowment of Orpheus as sculpted by Astrid Zydower.

It may interest you to know, but will probably not surprise you, that I frequently see young couples out of my window, the male with a camera and the female standing on the edge of the central fountain with her hand held up suggestively in front of Orpheus. I can only guess at what she is attempting to address.

If you warn me when you are likely to come again to Harewood, a visit which we should naturally anticipate with much pleasure, we will have the fountain filled a little fuller than usual and maybe some sinister fish deployed within it in order to withstand your assault on Orpheus and his endowment.

Yours sincerely

Lord Harewood

Chief Magistrate
Bow Street Magistrates Court
Bow Street
London

Dear Sir/Madam

I am writing to you as part of my quest for an unusual item; namely membership of the athletics club associated with the Bow Street Magistrates Court known as the Bow Street Runners.

Aged 42, I first began running almost 27 years ago as a rather chubby 15-year-old. At first my efforts were restricted to short road runs but soon developed into longer cross-country ventures and finally into long-distance fell races. I am sure that I am hooked to the fun that running brings but, apart from a £9 annual subscription to The Fell Runners Association, a national organisation that provides a fell-race agenda and a magazine, I have never actually become a member of any particular running club before.

Since the Bow Street Runners are so well known and are associated with a group of people recognised for their discipline and enforcement of order, I would be delighted to be considered for membership forthwith. I realise that there is a significant distance between Huddersfield, where I live, and Bow Street in London but the accolade of belonging to such a club would make the travelling to and fro a worthwhile task.

I would be most grateful if you could send to me the relevant membership application forms and would also like to take this opportunity to ask whether I need to purchase blue PT kit and a flashing light for winter evening training.

Many thanks for your time and consideration.

Sincerely

Michael A. Lee

Judge Penelope Hewitt
Senior District Judge (Chief Magistrate)

BOW STREET MAGISTRATES' COURT

LONDON WC2E 7AS

Tel: 020-7853-9232
Fax: 020-7853-9298

Mr M A Lee
Somewhere in West Yorkshire

22 May 2002

Dear Mr Lee

I was delighted to receive your letter of the 18th May and read about your achievements in running.

I am sorry to have to break the news to you that the Bow Street Runners no longer exists, the age and state of health of the District Judges was such that there was grave risk of injury to their health.

However, every cloud has a silver lining and this disappointment means you will not need to purchase all the equipment and the flashing light.

May I wish you every success in your fell running and cross-country ventures.

Yours sincerely

Penelope Hewitt.

Somewhere in West Yorkshire
26 May 2002

Head of Customer Services
Consignia PLC
148 Old Street
London EC1V 9HG

Dear Sir/Madam

I am writing to you as part of my quest for an unusual item; namely a 'Poetic Licence'.

Having spent a little time this afternoon wondering whom I might approach in my search for the aforementioned item, I came to the conclusion that, as the contemporary face of The Post Office which has had decades of selling and supplying various licences, you might be the ideal starting point in my enquiries.

While surfing the web I was most interested to read of the vast array of licence possibilities available within certain UK towns, ranging from dog-breeding and late-night café licences to pig-movement and scrap-metal-yard licences. There is, I notice, even a pool-betting licence available in some places, presumably for those who share a love of both the races and the swimming baths!

It seems that there are licences to cater for a substantially wide range of interests and tastes, business needs and hobbies, although many of these appear to be supplied by local-council departments. It was not immediately evident, however, whether there exists the opportunity for applying for and obtaining a poetic licence and I wondered if this was simply a quirk of the sites I visited or whether I was searching in the wrong places. I wonder if perhaps the good old established Post Office could shed more light on the subject!?

Having been both a writer and a salesman for quite some time, I often find myself in situations where exaggeration and focus seem to be par for the course and in this regard I wondered if it might be best to ensure that the claims I make in writing and in storytelling were protected by an officially purchased licence even if they are not actual objective facts. In this regard I would be most obliged for any advice and help you can provide in my quest for such an item.

I thank you in anticipation of your time and kind consideration in this matter and look forward to hearing from you in the very near future.

Sincerely

Michael A. Lee

31 May 2002

1-80000976

The new name for The Post Office Group

Mr M A Lee
Somewhere in West Yorkshire

Dear Mr Lee

Thank you for your letter of 29 May 2002 to Consignia plc Headquarters.

With regard to a "Poetic Licence" acquisition outlined in your letter, I refer to the Oxford English Dictionary " A poetic licence is a poet's or writer's departure from strict fact or correct grammar, for the sake of effect."

It is a phrase used to describe the use of exaggeration or storytelling in everyday life. Unfortunately, there is no "Official" licence of this sort provided by the Post Office.

I thank you for contacting Consignia plc.

Yours sincerely

Caroline Chaplin

Caroline Chaplin
Consignia Headquarters Customer Service Manager

Group Centre, 5th Floor, 148 Old Street, LONDON, EC1V 9HQ
Tel: 020 7250 2888 Fax: 020 7250 2030

Consignia plc is registered in England and Wales. Registered number 4138203. Registered office: 148 Old Street, LONDON. EC1V 9HQ.

Somewhere in West Yorkshire
28 May 2002
**cc Royal Society for the
Prevention of Cruelty to
Animals**

**Head of Enquiries
Battersea Dogs Home
4 Battersea Park Road
London SW8 4AA**

Dear Sir/Madam

I am writing to you as part of my quest for an unusual item; namely 'the hair of a dog'.

Although I have occasionally enjoyed a glass of beer or wine during the course of the last few years, rarely have I consumed sufficient to warrant any of the well-documented side effects that are described the next day by many people as 'hangovers'. *Au contraire*, my own meagre and infrequent ration of alcoholic beverage has usually created a certain sense of warmth and inner contentment during the evening of my self-indulgence, led me perhaps to the joyful and melodious singing of 'Danny Boy', and then created a pleasant fatigue conducive to a deep and restful night's sleep. By morning the alcohol has normally cleared from my system and I am fresh as the proverbial daisy, fully prepared to face a new and wonderful day.

Last Saturday, however, was an exception to the rule and it is for a related reason that I now write to you for help. Over the course of the evening I somehow consumed two flavoursome and fortifying glasses of a dark stout, a tumbler of homebrew mango wine and a little saké. I suspect that the host of the party that I was attending also added a little whisky to my cup of late-night cocoa.

As a consequence, next morning my head felt a little like a piece of two-by-two pine when it is placed in a vice for sanding, my mouth like the surface of the sandpaper had it been left out in the desert for a week or so and my sense of vitality similar to that of an inmate of Death Row. In short, my moderation of a lifetime was shaken and stirred, turned upside down and then punched. It took me almost three days to recover.

During my recovery period a friend suggested that should I obtain 'a hair of the dog' I might endure the symptoms of my self-induced suffering to a greater degree and make a swifter recovery than was the actual case. I did not manage to find one, however, as I do not own a dog and know few if any friends who do. Should I happen to experience a repeat of the foolish behaviour already described, however, I believe it would be prudent for me to obtain 'a hair of the dog' and keep it in my wallet or bathroom cabinet 'just in case'.

As a well-established organisation involved in the care of many different types of dog, I wondered if it might be possible for you to supply me with a hair of a dog proven to be of benefit in the circumstances I have described. My friend did not provide details about whether any specific breed of dog offered more success than another as far as hair was concerned, but if you believe that a German shepherd dog might provide a better hair than a poodle, or a terrier than a bulldog, in the provision of healing benefits, I will take your advice and, if convenient, an appropriate sample of hair as authoritative medical aid.

. . . continued

Many thanks indeed for your time and kind consideration and I look forward to hearing from you in the very near future.

Sincerely

Michael A. Lee

Battersea Dogs Home

Patron: Her Majesty The Queen
President: His Royal Highness Prince Michael of Kent

Mr M A Lee
Somewhere in West Yorkshire

4, Battersea Park Road, London SW8 4AA
Tel: 020-7622 3626   Fax: 020-7622 6451
www.dogshome.org

31st May 2002

Dear Mr Lee

Thank you for your letter, which we were delighted to receive.

I can certainly sympathise with the dreadful condition and symptoms that you have described and it would truly be a miracle of modern science if these could be alleviated at a faster rate than nature.

We usually find that the "Hair of the dog" treatment involved another alcoholic drink during the "morning after" suffering, and have no cases on file involving the consumption of a real dog's hair for this condition!

I am consequently sending you a selection of hairs taken from our groomer's dog brush and we would be delighted to hear back from you about any success that you encounter. We would however strongly suggest that this experiment be conducted steadily over a lengthy period of time, as we would never wish to cause you any further discomfort. We would also advise a consultation with your GP.

I would be happy to share the news of any success that you encounter with the staff at the Dogs Home. It would make a topical alternative to Aspirin or Resolve.

Yours sincerely

Head of Enquiries
Battersea Dogs Home

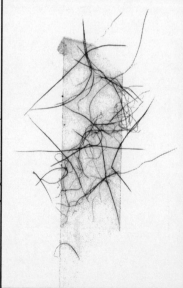

Battersea Dogs Home
4, Battersea Park Road,
London SW8 4AA
Tel: 020-7622 3626
Fax: 020-7622 6451

Battersea at Old Windsor
Priest Hill, Old Windsor,
Berkshire SL4 2JN
Tel: 01784 432929
Fax: 01784 471538

A Member of The Association of British Dogs and Cats Homes
Company Limited by Guarantee. Registered in England No. 278802   Registered as a Charity under
VAT Registration No. 726 5204 47 Registered Office: The Dogs Home Battersea, 4 Battersea P

Royal Society for the Prevention of Cruelty to Animals

Patron HM The Queen *Vice Patron* His Grace The Archbishop of Canterbury

Registered charity no. 219099

Our Ref: 2557669/chv

27 June 2002

Mr M A Lee
Somewhere in West Yorkshire

Dear Mr Lee

Thank you for your most unusual and poetic letter of 28 May. I apologise for the delay in replying and hope that in the meantime you have made a fine and full recovery from your evening of alcoholic indulgence.

I have pleasure in enclosing, as requested, a very special "hair of the dog" (indeed, a few!) most generously donated by our canine companion, Bailey, which, although unproven, may I hope prove useful to you in the event of any future occurrence of over-indulgence of the tippling variety. Please keep them in a safe place.

I am sure you will appreciate that the fulfilment of such rare and peculiar requests, whilst introducing a leavening element to an otherwise routine day of enquiry handling, places an unusual drain on the RSPCA's charitable resources, serving as in this case not the furtherance of the welfare of animals but the enhancement of the quality of human life. In token thereof, I hope you may consider this august organisation worthy of your future support and perhaps make application for an RSPCA affinity credit card or feel driven to make a small donation towards our future animal welfare work. I am therefore seizing the opportunity of enclosing a few leaflets which I hope may capture your interest.

A toast to your good health and to the welfare of all animals (and especially to Bailey, our doggie hair donor).

Yours sincerely

Caroline H Vodden (Mrs)
Head of Supporter Care

Royal Society for the Prevention of Cruelty to Animals

Patrons HM The Queen, HM Queen Elizabeth The Queen Mother *Vice Patron* His Grace The Archbishop of Canterbury

Registered charity no. 219099

"Hair of the dog"
from Bailey.

with compliments

Enquiries Service (Direct lines: Tel 0870 3335 999 Fax 0870 7530 284)

RSPCA Headquarters, Wilberforce Way, Southwater, Horsham, West Sussex RH13 7WN
Tel 0870 010 1181 Fax 0870 7530 284 DX 57628 HORSHAM 6 Website: http://www.rspca.org.uk

Somewhere in West Yorkshire
3 June 2002

Head of Customer Services
Thomas Crapper & Co
The Stable Yard
Alscot Park
Stratford-upon-Avon
Warwickshire CV37 8BL

Dear Sir/Madam

I am writing to you as part of my quest for an unusual item; namely the job title and suitable employment as 'A-Cistern Director' within a well-established waste-disposal solutions company. Since I chanced upon an advertisement for your own company within a magazine I was reading in a doctor's waiting room last week I decided that you might be the ideal place to begin my enquiries.

Aged 42, I have spent a significant amount of time in the vicinity of cisterns of the type you manufacture. As a matter of interest I have, since the age of 2, spent approximately 10 minutes each day or, if recalculated, 146,100 minutes, 2,435 hours, or 100 days and nights close to a variety of toilet cisterns and am therefore more than familiar with this range of products as far as appearance, mechanics and even colour schemes are concerned.

As an industrious and conscientious individual, I can assure you that I have a committed attitude to my various daily duties and I am known for my consistency and my regularity, which to some extent I am sure relies on my possession of adequate moral fibre.

I am a well-read and well-educated person, as the bookshelves in various rooms within my house would suggest, and pride myself as a traditionalist who has great respect for the great British institutions, a strong work ethic and successful organisation, as well as for our royal family and indeed our sovereign on the throne.

Should you be interested to consider me further for 'A-Cistern Director' I would be pleased to meet with you for interview and will be only too glad to bring with me a strong and very, very long CV for your perusal. (This, you will be glad to hear, is printed on soft and recycled paper to support the use of sustainable timber resources and to avoid the need to involve a drain-clearing company should the document be thoughtlessly discarded.)

Many thanks indeed for your time and kind consideration in regard to my hoped-for employment and I look forward to hearing from you in the very near future.

Sincerely

M. A. Lee

Michael A. Lee

THOMAS CRAPPER & COMPANY, LTD.

SANITARY ENGINEERS

By Warrant of Appointment to their Late Majesties Edward VII and George V.

ESTABLISHED 1861.   INCORPORATED 1904.   COMPANY No. 82482.

M. A. Lee, Esqᵃ,

Somewhere in West Yorkshire

8th June 1902.

Dear Mr Lee,

I am grateful to be in receipt of yours of the third instant, being an application for a situation at Crappers. My fellow directors and I have been much impressed to read your missive in all its detail. However this led us inexorably to the conclusion that you are greatly over-qualified for the post.

Therefore I regret to relate that we are unable to offer a position to you but we wish you well in your endeavours. You might try Messrs Boggs & Co. of Looe, Cornwall.

I am, yours sincerely,

Simon Kirby.

THE STABLE YARD,   ALSCOT PARK,   STRATFORD-ON-AVON,   WARWICKSHIRE.   (CV37 8BL)

ELECTRIC MESSAGES: wc@thomas-crapper.com   TELEPHONE: ALDERMINSTER (01789) 450 522.

MANAGING DIRECTOR – S.P.J. KIRBY.   FACSIMILE: "   "   "   "   523.

The President
Camberwell Society
38 Camberwell Grove
Camberwell

Dear Sir/Madam

I am writing to you as part of my quest for an unusual item; namely an opportunity to meet a world-famous 'Camberwell Beauty'.

It is with a certain degree of regret that I look back over the last 20 years to the countless organisations to which I have belonged and from which I have resigned, which have been unable to point me in the direction of anything more than Painted Ladies in Pontefract and fragile Lacewings in Halifax. So many of my past leads have offered neither the charms, character nor looks of my expectations and consequently they have simply fluttered by on damaged wings or on flight paths quite different to my own journey through life.

As a northern man living in the town of Huddersfield I am not familiar with the Camberwell area nor of places locally where a Camberwell Beauty might be seen and so I am writing to you for your kind help and advice.

I would be grateful if you could recommend places I could visit where I might observe the 'Beauty' of my dreams and so permit my adding the consequent encounter to my trusty logbook. This is at present collecting dust on an office shelf and looking more and more like a large cocoon each day.

Doubtless you have many similar requests concerning the search for a Camberwell Beauty and I thank you for your time and kind consideration in this matter.

I look forward to hearing from you in the very near future.

Sincerely

Michael A. Lee

Mr M A Lee
Somewhere in West Yorkshire

12th June 2002

Dear Sir,

Thank you for your letter of June 2nd.

As I imagine you will not be surprised to learn, I am not sure whether in your letter you are by Camberwell Beauties referring to butterflies or women. If the former, I will try and make enquiries to find out. If the latter, I suggest you either place an advertisement in the Society's journal - the Camberwell Quarterly - or move to Camberwell and join the Society where several of our members in my opinion deserve this accolade.

So far as the Quarterly is concerned I don't think we have ever before carried general invitations to particular social encounters with members of the opposite sex but if tastefully drafted and likely to cause no offence I daresay the Editor might be willing to publish one.

Yours faithfully,

Conrad Dehn

Somewhere in West Yorkshire
10 June 2002

Head of Customer Services
Wilkinson
JK House
Roebuck Way
Manton Wood
Worksop
Nottinghamshire S80 3YY

Dear Sir/Madam

I am writing to you as part of my quest for an unusual item; namely a 'corporate ladder'. I thought that, as a large retail organisation involved in the sale of a wide range of do-it-yourself and gardening equipment, you might be able to advise me.

Over recent months there has been much reference at the company for which I work to individuals who have gained promotion in their various careers, and indeed salary increases also, as a consequence of their 'climbing the corporate ladder'.

Although I have worked consistently hard at my job and been rewarded in a reasonable and satisfactory manner for my efforts to date, I would be keen to move even further forward in my employment and am eager to obtain one of the aforementioned corporate ladders for this purpose.

I have never actually seen a corporate ladder and thought that rather than showing my ignorance and asking one of my management team where I would find one I ought first to make enquiries elsewhere. The added benefit of this approach is that it avoids the possible scenario of my making a calculated guess at purchasing a corporate ladder from someone such as yourselves but making a mistake and bringing home a step-ladder or roofing ladder instead.

Doubtless you receive many similar letters to this over the course of the year and so I thank you for your time and kind consideration and look forward to hearing from you in the very near future, telling me where I might purchase such an item.

Sincerely

M. A. Lee

Michael A. Lee

Wilkinson

JK House
PO Box 20
Roebuck Way
Manton Wood
Worksop
Nottinghamshire
S80 3YY
Tel: (01909) 505505
Fax: (01909) 505777

Mr M A Lee
Somewhere in West Yorkshire

Our ref: 97090/02BOSWORD   17 June 2002

Dear Mr Lee

Thank you for your recent enquiry regarding your quest for a 'corporate' ladder.

I too have heard many references to such an item and, like you, have been attracted to the benefits that such an item appears to bring. Those who own one clearly enjoy the positive outcomes that can be gained – indeed I've found that people who must own a corporate ladder of their own are reluctant to lend me theirs even for a week or two. I can sympathise with your predicament in not wanting to show your ignorance by asking your management as I know from experience the unusually vacant expression and strange reply that one can get from making such enquiries.

However, only a few months ago I believed that I had made some progress and actually acquired a corporate ladder of my very own, but this turned out to be one of the older models of the 'corporate kick-step' and so my personal search continues.

I am aware that our buying team is currently working hard in the Far East, searching for a supplier who is willing to trade openly in the market of corporate ladders. I understand that there are difficulties however, as in line with our marketing strategy such a product must be available for us to sell at the most competitive price and be of the highest quality. Our understanding of this product is that it must be handled and used with the greatest of care, for not only can it be climbed, but one can also fall off (or indeed be pushed). Therefore, the buyer's search is complicated by the need to risk-assess every product sample to evaluate its safety.

I am sorry that on this occasion I am unable to help any further and wish you well in your own search for a corporate ladder. In the meantime, may I suggest purchasing Wilko Broad Beans at 89p as an alternative, as perhaps an almighty beanstalk will develop, enabling you to achieve your dreams another way.

Many thanks for your letter and best wishes in your quest.

Assuring you of our best attention at all times.

Yours sincerely
pp WILKINSON

David Bosworth
<u>Customer Relations Manager</u>

REGISTERED No. 365335 ENGLAND.   PARENT COMPANY WILKINSON HARDWARE STORES LTD.
SUBSIDIARIES WILKINSON HARDWARE STORES (LEICESTER) LTD. S.C. HARDWARES LTD.
WILKINSON BROS. (HANDSWORTH) LTD. L.M. COOPER & CO. LTD.

POSITIVE ABOUT DISABLED PEOPLE

INVESTOR IN PEOPLE

Somewhere in West Yorkshire
10 June 2002

Head of Enquiries
College of Optometrists
42 Craven Street
London WC2N 5NG

Dear Sir/Madam

I am writing to you as part of my quest for an unusual item; namely a pair of 'context lenses'.

For many years I have suffered from a degree of myopia or short-sightedness and would like to take this opportunity to mention that I have been very pleased with Boots Opticians both for offering me an excellent eye-testing service during this time and for providing me with various high quality lenses and indeed spectacle frames when required. It is with reference to another area of vision, however, that I write today. Let me explain.

Although I am perfectly capable of observing physical detail at a distance through my everyday glasses or, if out of the normal range of vision, through my handy binoculars, as well as being capable of reading easily and performing the full range of tasks that require watching objects close to the eyes I am, on occasion, challenged to position things in context.

My understanding of the relative importance of various issues and priorities at home and at work as well as during various aspects of social life is sometimes exaggerated and poorly focused. The complexity of everyday life with its countless demands is often unclear to me and at times significantly blurred around the edges.

It is for this reason I would find it enormously helpful to acquire the aforementioned context lenses so that my sense of perspective is restored and I can see life for what it really is. As the College of Optometrists, I thought that you might be the ideal starting point for my enquiries!

Doubtless you receive many letters of this kind on a regular basis and so I thank you for your time and consideration and look forward to hearing from you in the near future.

Sincerely

M. A. Lee

Michael A. Lee

THE COLLEGE OF OPTOMETRISTS

Mr M A Lee
Somewhere in West Yorkshire

24th July 2002

Dear Mr. Lee,

Thank you for your letter which has been passed to me.

I am very interested to hear of your request, as I too would find such lenses useful on occasion. They would go well with my Round Tuit. Unfortunately the College is unable to help you in your search, but you may find that the British Context Lens Association (www.bcla.org.uk) will be able to give you more information.

Please let me know if you succeed in your quest.

Kind regards

Yours sincerely

Dr. Susan Blakeney
Optometric Adviser

42 Craven Street, London WC2N 5NG
Tel 020 7839 6000
optometric.adviser@college-optometrists.org

Somewhere in West Yorkshire
19 June 2002

Jill Silander-Hatch
Garden Gifts of Distinction
32 Beaconsfield Way
Frome
Somerset BA11 2UD

Dear Sir/Madam

I am writing to you as part of my quest for an unusual item; namely a 'Fountain of Eternal Youth'.

Since turning 40 a couple of years ago, I have become increasingly conscious of the way in which my face is wrinkling, my joints are beginning to ache after exercise and my ears and nose are sprouting wiry hairs. It is certainly becoming more difficult for me to maintain a balance between the enjoyment of good food and an acceptable physique and I also find it an impossible task to retain more than a token amount of hair on the top of my head.

Names and places that were once readily available to my system of mental recollection often evade me now and only yesterday I accidentally put on my dressing gown on top of my shirt and tie instead of the desired jacket. In short, my ageing process has kicked in with a vengeance. It is in this regard, therefore, that I write to you.

Surfing the net last night I chanced upon your website advertising, among other things, a range of fountains and wondered with great hope if your range might include that most English of ancient artefacts, a 'fountain of eternal youth'. I can already imagine such a fountain positioned appropriately in the back garden of my home here in Huddersfield, offering an experience of aesthetic worth as well as readily available draughts of age-repelling and life-preserving water.

Doubtless such a fountain will be highly coveted and priced accordingly but may I emphasise to you my substantial interest in acquiring such an item to hasten the day my appearance and physical prowess return to that of my late teens and early twenties.

Many thanks indeed for your time and kind consideration and I look forward to hearing from you in the very near future.

Sincerely

M. A. Lee

Michael A. Lee

Garden Gifts of Distinction

32 Beaconsfield Way FROME Somerset BA11 2UD
Tel: *(01373) 471749* **Fax:** *(01373) 303113* **Email:** *Gardengiftsfrome@aol.com*
www.Gardengiftsofdistinction.com

Birdbaths - Statues - Sconces - Pedestals - Planters
Plaques & Urns for Gardens, Patios,
Courtyards & Conservatories

20th September 2002

Mr M A Lee
Somewhere in West Yorkshire

Dear Mr Lee

It is with sorrow that I reply to your letter of
the 19th June. I have spent from then till now
testing all my fountains to see if one would meet
your requirements of "Fountain of Eternal Youth".
Though they are all aesthetically beautiful, none
have returned me to my girlhood!

However, gazing at these delightful fountains has
made me realise that youth is not everything! An
appreciation of beauty grows with age - so the
fountains appear more beautiful & ageless though we
do not!

So do return to my website - and order a fountain
today!

Yours sincerely

(Mrs) Jill Silander-Hatch

Distinctive Gifts for the Discerning

VAT No: 753 6910 16

67

Somewhere in West Yorkshire
19 June 2002

Head of Customer Services
Environment & Transportation Service
Kirklees Metropolitan Council
Flint Street
Fartown
Huddersfield HD1 6LG

Dear Sir/Madam

I am writing to you as part of my quest for an unusual item; namely a solution to my present state of 'writer's block'.

Over the last couple of years I have spent an hour or more each evening compiling with great satisfaction a range of creative and grammatically colourful pieces of written material designed to entertain, stimulate and inspire even the most unimaginative hearts and minds of potential readers.

Each day I would see another two or three pages of wonderful word sculpture appear before me as if by magic and I would retire to bed happy with my literary effusions and fall into the deep and refreshing sleep that comes only from true contentment and perceived achievement.

Sadly, however, I must inform you that during the previous few days I have unfortunately developed a 'writer's block' with the result that my adjectives have become sluggish, my nouns full of inertia, my analogies without momentum. My whole system of creative writing has ground to an unexplained and frustrating halt. It is for this reason that I write in desperation to your good selves.

As a well-established service experienced in the art and science of unblocking pipes and drains, I wondered if you might be able to offer any practical solutions to rid me of my writer's block, ensuring that the sentences and paragraphs that have flown so freely in times past are once again allowed to move in an unhindered fashion and find their intended outlet?

Doubtless, the key to survival in the competitive world of business in these hectic times has much to do with innovative application of existing techniques. I decided I would seek a solution from a team of experts who are used to dealing with the difficulties that often lie just around the bend and whose tools have the characteristics of both flexibility and versatility.

I daresay that you receive many enquiries of this kind on a regular basis and so I thank you for your time and kind consideration and look forward to hearing from you in the very near future.

Sincerely

Michael A. Lee

Kirklees
METROPOLITAN • COUNCIL

ENVIRONMENT & TRANSPORTATION SERVICE

Highway Network Manager
Richard Bunney

Flint Street
Fartown
Huddersfield HD1 6LG
West Yorkshire

Please contact:- Mr F O'Dwyer
Tel: 01484 225529

E-mail: frank.o'dwyer@kirkleesmc.gov.uk
Fax: 01484 225599
Text phone for deaf people: 01484 225531

Our Ref: 3.3.1/HIM043947/FO'D/CAH   Date: 24 June 2002
Your Ref: None

Mr M A Lee
Somewhere in West Yorkshire

Dear Mr Lee

RE: WRITER'S BLOCK

I refer to your letter dated 19 June asking for help with 'Writers' Block'

I must start by explaining that I am nowhere near as eloquent as you; it isn't in the requirements or training for engineers.

I don't feel qualified to offer a solution, but I would like to try and offer an insight and suggest some sources for you to explore.

It is at once understandable and intriguing that you link your problem with ours in maintaining the highway drainage system.

Early work by such people as d'Arcy and Bernoulli derived algorithms to describe the functioning of drainage systems.

For many years there has been a popular understanding of the 'stream of consciousness', perhaps this has encouraged people to think of the working of the brain in similar terms to the working of drains.

However there is no comparison in complexity. Consciousness has been described as 'The last great mystery of science'.

Continued over/....

1405JUN.DOC

Terry Brown - Highways and Transportation Manager

INVESTOR IN PEOPLE

Researchers are beginning to question the accepted concept of a stream of experiences passing through the mind. Perhaps this concept has been thought of as similar to gravity driving water through a drain.

Susan Blackmore has recently suggested that consciousness may be an illusion, so if it isn't what it seems, no wonder it is proving such a mystery.

'The Hard Problem' as David Chalmers calls it is 'how can the firing of brain cells produce subjective experience? It seems like turning water in to wine'

Several researchers are working on projects. For example Francis Crick is trying to pin down how brain activity corresponds to the world we see and Susan Greenfield is looking for the particular physical state of the brain which accompanies a subjective feeling.

Accessible sources you may try are New Scientist and Scientific American. The Meme Machine, by Blackmore and a recent Scientific American special edition 'The Hidden Mind' may also provide some insight and possibly inspiration for you.

Understanding the process is one thing but perhaps you would consider maintenance of the brain as well. Two recent items of interest are that the US Environmental Protection Agency have confirmed that burning candles with wicks stiffened by being treated with lead release high levels of lead throughout the house. All candles manufactured in America or Western Europe use alternatives. You will be aware of the effect of lead particles in the air. A small study at Kings College hints at a beneficial effect from eating a diet high in soya.

If, after following up these links, the insight they provide into the working of the brain does not inspire the clearing of the current blockage, perhaps you could accept a challenge and pen 1,500 words on why 'Flying a kite at night is so weird'.

In closing, I must explain that the main function of the brain is to manage resources and, interesting as this may be on a quiet Sunday, it isn't possible to use the Authority's Highways resources on continuing the correspondence. Perhaps you could consider enrolling on a creative writing course. I will leave that as another research item for you.

Best of luck.

Yours sincerely

FRANK O'DWYER
Group Engineer, Maintenance.

1405JUN.DOC

Somewhere in West Yorkshire
19 June 2002

Dr P. Faulkner
Field Head Surgery
Leymoor Road
Golcar
Huddersfield HD7 4QQ

Dear Dr Faulkner

I am writing to you as a part of my quest for an unusual item; namely information about a condition mentioned to me by a friend who has recently completed a period of work at Sizewell Power Station. I thought you might be able to suggest some possible treatment options for a condition that sounds particularly distressing and one which I am convinced I am also suffering from myself.

When my friend mentioned 'The China Syndrome' I had imbibed at least five pints of a rather smooth and palatable real ale, but I nevertheless distinctly remember him mentioning extremely high temperatures and their affect on physical stability as a consequence of this state. I am sure that he told me that the syndrome had critical consequences and was something that should cause a huge degree of concern to all involved.

When last Tuesday I myself began to feel rather hot and feverish, with a significant sinking feeling, I was not convinced that a mere self-limiting virus was to blame; rather this was another manifestation of 'The China Syndrome.' Unfortunately, I am unable to find out anything more from my small collection of medical textbooks and presume that even my two volumes of *The Oxford Textbook of Medicine* may be out of date. I can tell you, however, that I feel urgently in need of advice before the symptoms become unmanageable and I find myself resting below ground for time immemorial.

Once again many thanks for your time and kind consideration and I look forward to hearing from you in the very near future.

Sincerely

Michael A. Lee

FIELDHEAD SURGERY
Dr. PETER FAULKNER
Dr. OWEN DEMPSEY
Dr. MICHAEL WALLWORK
Dr. SHEILA BENETT
Telephone: (01484) 654504
Fax: (01484) 460296
e-mail: fieldhead@doctors.org.uk

FIELD HEAD
LEYMOOR ROAD
GOLCAR
HUDDERSFIELD
HD7 4QQ

Our Ref; PF/kg

21st June, 2002

Mr M. A. Lee
Somewhere in West Yorkshire

Dear Mr. Lee,

I read your letter of 19th June 2002 with interest. I have studied your symptoms and have come to the conclusion that the nearest equivalent of a viral illness which you correctly assume, is that of the 'Kawasaki' syndrome. This causes fevers and general malaise with the possibility of sudden, if not, later death from coronary artery involvement. I am fairly sure that this is not the case for you as, I believe, you have no interest in motorcycles and there is certainly no illness known as the 'Japan' syndrome.

I have discovered that the 'China' syndrome is indeed a possibility in your case, as the dysmorphic physiognomy which you possess may have been produced by non-subtle genetic modification through some form of irradiation. I have based this possibility of severe radiation exposure from the fact that you are almost completely bald and it is well known that the hair follicles are particularly radio sensitive.

The disaster scenario of rapidly approaching death is unlikely to be avoided, unless a heroine can be found to rescue you from your plight before total melt-down occurs.

I am glad that you are able to have five pints of your real ale, as I am sure that the time is approaching where you will be completely unable to drink when your gastrointestinal system is stripped of its lining from radiation effects.

I hope that your last days are comfortable but I can be of help, in that I am aware of a number of excellent joiners who should be able to make a coffin suitable for your requirements.

All the best.

Yours sincerely,

Dr P. Faulkner.

Somewhere in West Yorkshire
27 June 2002

Dr P. Faulkner
Field Head Surgery
Leymoor Road
Golcar
Huddersfield HD7 4QQ

Dear Dr Faulkner

First and foremost may I take this opportunity to thank you for your kind help with reference to my enquiries regarding 'The China Syndrome.'

Having considered the rather gloomy prospects associated with a confirmed diagnosis of 'The China Syndrome' I have looked closely and at length at various other aspects of my current symptomatology, hoping to find a less pessimistic prognosis. Once again, I would appreciate your advice in this matter.

I am beginning to wonder whether my original fears of complete meltdown were unwarranted but am still at somewhat of a loss to explain the following physical manifestations. Let me explain.

Several friends and colleagues have recently pointed out to me that I have a 'brass neck' and am sometimes 'hot headed'. I have certainly been known to 'see red' especially concerning the roll-out of unreasonable company expectations by various members of the senior management team and, when addressing issues connected to the above, have been accused of having a 'nose for trouble'. Doubtless my sharing of these unfortunate medical phenomena would also suggest that I tend to 'wear my heart on my sleeve'.

As a consequence of recognising such a miscellany of disturbing presentations I am now thoroughly confused and am not sure whether I ought to be referred to a neurologist, orthopaedic surgeon, specialist in opthalmology, a clinician in ENT or a cardio-thoracic expert.

I would be grateful for any light you can shed on such an unusual case-history as mine and look forward to hearing from you in the very near future.

Sincerely

Michael A. Lee

FIELDHEAD SURGERY
Dr. PETER FAULKNER
Dr. OWEN DEMPSEY
Dr. MICHAEL WALLWORK
Dr. SHEILA BENETT
Telephone: (01484) 654504
Fax: (01484) 460296
e-mail: fieldhead@doctors.org.uk

FIELD HEAD
LEYMOOR ROAD
GOLCAR
HUDDERSFIELD
HD7 4QQ

Our Ref; PF/kg

4th July, 2002

Mr M. A. Lee
Somewhere in West Yorkshire

Dear Michael,

Many thanks for your letter of 27th June 2002. I am afraid that I am not able to be more forthcoming in the possibility of a better outcome with your condition. The position of chaos in to which your body appears to be descending may indeed lead your friends and colleagues to note the fact that you do indeed have a brass neck – this may be easily be put down to the fact that there may be some transition from base materials in to brass - and undoubtedly, your body is made up of extremely base material. I can only assume that colleagues have noticed that you are hot headed due to the lack of insulation on top of your scalp, such that any thermal emission will be completely unhindered.

As mentioned before, bleeding from several sites may cause you to see red if you are stricken with a conjunctival haemorrhage and as for having a nose for trouble, should the condition progress, then you may lose your nose altogether, hence not be troubled with people accusing you of having one of these items.

I am sure the fact that you wish to wear your heart on your sleeve may be indicative of some severe psychological disturbance and hallucinogenic problems induced by many pints of real ale, which will no doubt cause hallucinations of the appearance of various internal organs on exterior parts of your body. This line of reasoning may also account for the fact that you may have, at times, appeared legless.

I can only commiserate with your sad condition and hope that you do take my advice as outlined in the original letter to make yourself comfortable in the short time that you have left upon this Earth, before total disorganisation of your system takes place.

I am sure you have gathered from our correspondence that I regard your condition as completely unique, as indeed I am sure there is only one of a kind with reference to yourself.

Yours sincerely,

Dr. P. Faulkner.

Somewhere in West Yorkshire
18 July 2002

Dr P. Faulkner
Field Head
Leymoor Road
Golcar
Huddersfield HD7 4QQ

Dear Dr Faulkner

Once again may I take this opportunity to thank you for your time and kind consideration in your advice about my broad-ranging miscellaneous presentations as previously described.

I was understandably concerned, though not surprised, to hear that mine is a rather unique condition but have come to the conclusion that, despite the inevitability of the complete disorganisation and eventual meltdown of my physical being, I ought to apply my remaining time to helping other people as best I can. In this regard I am writing a letter of concern related to my dear wife and would again be most grateful for your learned advice and suggestions. I wondered specifically if there might be a suitable treatment regime for a problem with which my wife is currently afflicted, specifically a 'bone of contention'.

Almost every day during the last few months my wife has approached me with a look of sheer agony on her face and a sense of despair in her voice and has exclaimed: 'I have a bone of contention to discuss with you.' I am never quite sure how she manages to move off at a conversational tangent from this musculo-skeletal problem to various shortfalls in my own behaviour and to my various unfinished household and garden tasks and tie the two irreversibly together but it is clear that her suffering is affecting her judgement to a significant degree.

I myself have suffered considerably in the past from low back pain and recall gaining substantial benefit from physiotherapy and massage. I wondered if perhaps my wife might also receive help from a suitably qualified physiotherapist, osteopath or chiropractor so that this 'bone of contention' of hers is manipulated in such a way as to put it to rest once and for all.

Although I have attempted to find the aforementioned bone in my books of human anatomy and indeed on the Internet I have to date been unsuccessful. I am wondering whether my wife is using a local term for what others generally know as 'the funny bone' or perhaps 'the humorous' or whether her description is completely disjointed or even requires a certain amount of reconstruction.

Many thanks indeed for your time and kind consideration in this sensitive matter and I look forward to hearing from you in the very near future.

Sincerely

M. A. Lee

Michael A. Lee

FIELDHEAD SURGERY
Dr. PETER FAULKNER
Dr. OWEN DEMPSEY
Dr. MICHAEL WALLWORK
Dr. SHEILA BENETT
Telephone: (01484) 654504
Fax: (01484) 460296
e-mail: fieldhead@doctors.org.uk

FIELD HEAD
LEYMOOR ROAD
GOLCAR
HUDDERSFIELD
HD7 4QQ

Our Ref; PF/kg

24th July, 2002

Mr M. A. Lee
Somewhere in West Yorkshire

Dear Michael,

How pleasant it was to hear from you again.

I will have to start charging for giving my professional opinion as I realise that I have been giving it far too freely to date.

You have correctly identified a peculiar anatomical variant present in the female of the species, which is the "bone of contention". This is an interesting ossification found in a very secretive area in the female body.

The origin of this article may be traced to Biblical times, when Adam had a piece of rib removed from his body from which to fashion his partner, Eve. It is apparent that God did not quite manage to fashion an identical skeleton from this, leaving an extra particle which subsequently became the bone of contention.

Although the bone of contention is rarely exhibited, indications of its presence may be given during times of intense annoyance and frustration, hence it is easy to see why your wife is on the point of disclosing its presence more fully.

Management of the bone of contention would be rather drastic, in as much as it would involve a spousectomy to remove the source of annoyance. In your case, this may not be necessary, as your condition does appear to be imminently fatal, so this unpleasant surgical procedure may be dispensed with. Massage does help, giving great pleasure to the woman concerned, but as to whether it is actually a valid treatment for the bone is another matter.

I can reassure you that the bone of contention as an anatomical entity is certainly not the funny bone or humerus and represents a serious development in anatomical study.

I hope my description of the bone of contention is of help to you.

Yours sincerely,

Dr. P. Faulkner.

Somewhere in West Yorkshire
19 June 2002

Head of Customer Services
White Knight
72 George Street
Caversham
Reading
Berkshire RG4 8DW

Dear Sir/Madam

I am writing to you as part of my quest for an unusual item; namely the services of a dry-cleaning organisation that is able and willing to launder my money.

Over the years I have taken my various two-piece suits to a whole range of dry cleaners conveniently located near the homes I have owned or rented. In the majority of cases my suits have been returned to me in immaculate condition and I have been able to present myself at work in a smart and dapper manner.

The same is true of various pairs of casual trousers and indeed also when the occasional need for my curtains to be dry cleaned has arisen. Stains have vanished, creases and folds have been banished and the dust and grime of everyday life have been replaced with a pleasing cleanliness and restoration of the appearance of something new.

In this regard I wondered if you might be able similarly to launder some of the £5, £10 and £20 notes that come regularly and legitimately into my possession but are creased and wrinkled, often dirty and lacking the lustre that one ideally expects of paper currency. There is nothing worse than filthy lucre!

I have certainly heard of various companies and institutions that launder money but sadly cannot find such a reference in *Yellow Pages*. Logic suggests to me that laundering is surely a function of the dry-cleaning industry and this explains the rationale for my writing to you in this regard, especially since you bare the gallant name of 'White Knight' and will probably come galloping to my rescue with much-needed help as soon as possible.

Doubtless you receive many letters along similar lines to this and so I thank you for your time and kind consideration and look forward to hearing from you in the very near future.

Sincerely

M. A. Lee

Michael A. Lee

White Night Laundry Services Ltd
72 George Street
Caversham
Reading
Berkshire RG4 8DW

20 June 2002

Michael. A. Lee
Somewhere in West Yorkshire

Dear Michael

Thank you for the opportunity to be of service to you.

White Night Laundry Services Ltd is able and willing to launder your money immediately.
Please send by return of post a very large package containing as many £5, £10 and £20 notes as you can get into a suitcase or large laundry box.
We promise to launder your money but cannot guarantee to return it to you.

Do you require the above items to be dry cleaned or washed and pressed if they are as dirty and creased and wrinkled as you suggest?

Awaiting an early reply

Somewhere in West Yorkshire
24 June 2002

Head of Enquiries
British Weight Lifters' Association
131 Hurst Street
Oxford OX4 1HE

Dear Sir/Madam

I am writing to you as part of my quest for an unusual item; namely the services of one of your members capable of lifting a weight from my mind.

Doubtless you would agree with me that we live in an era where life is generally lived by a large proportion of the British population at a far faster pace than ever before. Despite the innumerable leaps forward in home comforts, hi-technology and indeed in medicine, many individuals apply themselves so intensely to the everyday challenges of careers, sports, social and family life that they are often in danger of over-stressing themselves and sometimes even experiencing the so-called 'burn-out syndrome'. I may well be one of these individuals.

Aged 42, I am one of society's many 'task jugglers', attempting to maintain a fine balance between responsibilities and duties at home and at work. As a result I have for some time now experienced the common problem of having much to think about. It all weighs very heavily indeed upon my mind.

Despite trying various relaxation techniques and distractions such as drum beating, making jams and talking to herbaceous perennials in my back garden, I still find it hard to switch off and put aside my many mental burdens. It is in this regard that I write.

Rather than experiment further with various avenues of stress management, I thought I would ask whether you know of a person who is so strong that they could simply lift the weight from my mind and carry it somewhere far from my focus and attention.

I am sure that you receive many enquiries of a similar nature to this and so I thank you for your time and kind consideration and look forward to hearing from you in the very near future with appropriate advice and suggestions.

Sincerely

M. A. Lee

Michael A. Lee

British Weight Lifters' Association

Grovenor House
131 Hurst Street
Oxford OX4 1HE

Mr M A Lee
Somewhere in West Yorkshire

1st July 2002

Dear Mr Lee

Thank you for your letter of 24th June.

I regret that as we are a voluntary body, and rely on a limited number of volunteers to help us, we are not in a position to be able to assist with your particular enquiry.

Yours sincerely

J Gaul

Somewhere in West Yorkshire
28 June 2002

Director
Natural History Museum
Ipswich

Dear Sir/Madam

I am writing to you as part of my quest for an unusual item; namely official recognition as 'The Long-Lost Missing Link' by the Natural History Museum in Ipswich.

Aged 42, I have for many years been rather concerned at the extent and thickness of my ginger-brown body hair which sits like a doormat across my chest, back, arms and shoulders as well as my legs and, indeed, the soles of my feet. Just recently this preponderance of reasonably soft human fur has been joined by some coarser cousins in my ears and nostrils and, when viewed in profile together with my receding forehead and heavily set eyebrows, does tend to present a rather unlikely modern man.

As a longstanding member of the Fell Runners Association there is nothing I like better than to run through the ancient oak woods and peat bogs of Yorkshire in England and, when the spirit takes me, to sing the odd song. Fellow runners suggest that these are mere grunts and howls of a primeval nature.

I am thrilled when I spot on the hilltops a rabbit or mountain hare and have been known to leave the race at hand to pursue with great glee these small edible creatures as if driven by an uncontrollable but integral part of my inner self. I have no great interest in the comforts and hi-technology of modern life and am quite content sleeping beneath the stars or wandering over rocky crag and green dale.

Over the last few months there have been many occasions when I have been pursued by vicious-looking dogs who moments before seeing me were happily enjoying a juicy bone or playing with their master's toddler. My wife has suggested that one possible explanation is that I probably look and smell rather primitive to the dogs and consequently their own natures revert to those times long ago when wolves and tribal man were sworn enemies. In short, she has suggested I am a little different from other contemporary men and may indeed be a throwback to a more ancient time. I am inclined to agree with her!

If then you wish to meet with me for the purposes of an interview and an assessment for validation purposes, confirming my status as an individual displaying the physical and certain cultural traits of early Neanderthal man or perhaps even an example of *Dinanthropoides nivalis*, then please contact me as soon as is conveniently possible. I am more than happy to appear at your museum as an exhibit.

I thank you for your time and kind consideration of this letter of enquiry and look forward to hearing from you in the very near future.

Sincerely

Michael A. Lee

Ipswich Borough Council Museums & Galleries High Street Ipswich IP1 3QH
Telephone: 01473 433550   Facsimile: 01473 433558
Email: museums.service@ipswich.gov.uk   Website: www.ipswich.gov.uk
Minicom: 01473 432526

Please ask for:

Our Ref: David Lampard

Directline: DJL/JRF [5.3.1]
              22 July 2002

IPSWICH

BOROUGH
COUNCIL

Mr M A Lee
Somewhere in West Yorkshire

Tim Heyburn
BA PGCE AMA
Head of Museums

Dear Mr Lee

Thank you for your letter regarding your status as "The long lost missing link". Unfortunately I do not feel that I have the necessary expertise to comment on your status as I am a marine biologist by training. Also Ipswich Museum does not possess the resources to carry out the more detailed study that your case warrants. At the least this seems to suggest some sort of DNA analysis by a larger institution.

However you have raised a few interesting points. You do not say between what species that you believe you are the long lost missing link between. There are a number of possibilities; the Neanderthals for example are a distinct species and there is only some recent slightly controversial suggestions that they possibly interbred with modern humans in Spain. There are a number of other hominid ancestors, however recreating their physical attributes is a theoretical business.

However it is well known that humans share more than 90% of our genetic material with the other primates and the Orang Utan for example has coarse orangey hair, although it is relatively slow moving and tends to be vegetarian.

Have you discovered whether any other people in Huddersfield have developed the same characteristics?   your condition may be part of a local cluster and other examples may allow some sort of statistical analysis to be carried out.

Unfortunately Huddersfield is outside of our collecting area and we are unable to take up your suggestion of appearing as an exhibit. Have you tried museums nearer to your home area. The other problem is that we do not have a licence to exhibit live specimens. Our other specimens are of course stuffed and mounted, which is a permanent, not to say drastic step to take.

I am sorry that I cannot help you any further with your quest. However, good luck in your search.

Yours sincerely

David J Lampard

David Lampard
(*Keeper Natural Sciences*)
Ipswich Borough Council Museums Service

This information can be made
available on audio tape, braille or
alternative formats upon request
from the above telephone number

Animal Welfare
Benefits
Housing Advisory Services
Ipswich Borough Homes
Local Tax
Sport and Play
Strategic Planning & Regeneration

Chief Executive: James D Hehir
Directors: Laurence Collins, Tracey Lee, Michael J Palmer
Printed on environmentally friendly paper

Somewhere in West Yorkshire
5 July 2002

Professor Ian Tracey
Chorus Master
Royal Liverpool Philharmonic
Hope Street
Liverpool L1 9BP

Dear Professor

I am writing to you as part of my quest for an unusual item; namely a 'human dawn chorus' here in the garden of my home in Huddersfield.

Despite the fact that the English summer has numerous days that begin very early in the morning with the first hint of light at 4.00 a.m., when magnificent dawn choruses are provided by every neighbourhood bird with an ear and beak for music, I inevitably sleep through the entertainment and wake around 7.00 a.m. Should I wake any earlier I fear that my sleep deficit would interfere with my demanding work and make the already stretching challenges a more difficult burden to bear.

Unfortunately, this has meant the development of a profound and ongoing sense of loss as I have been missing out on what I believe can be a most uplifting and almost spiritual winged concert. I am now looking for viable and more conveniently timed reproductions. It is in this regard that I write to your good self as primary contact for the Royal Liverpool Philharmonic.

I wondered if there might be a chance that the accomplished members of your choir could put some time aside early one morning in the next few weeks, travel over to my garden in Huddersfield and sing a selection of appropriate harmonious songs to which I might awake with pleasure and contentment. Perhaps the choir could begin with 'Morning has Broken', move on to the old favourite, 'Sunshine on my Shoulder', and finish the medley with 'The Leaving of Liverpool'.

Although I am not a wealthy man and cannot offer any financial reward for such a favour, I can guarantee endless coffee and croissants and I assume that many of the neighbours will join with me in astonished applause as they look out of their bedroom windows to see 116 choir members singing to their hearts' content on my back lawn.

I have no doubt that you are inundated with many requests of this kind and so I thank you for your time and kind consideration in relation to this matter and look forward to hearing from you in the very near future.

Sincerely

Michael A. Lee

P.S. There is usually ample parking capacity for your coaches and minibuses at the side of the road at the top of the cul-de-sac in which the house is situated.

P.P.S. Please let me know approximately how many croissants you will require.

Royal Liverpool Philharmonic

Mr M A Lee
Somewhere in West Yorkshire

12 July 2002

Dear Mr Lee,

Thank you for your letter. The RLPC is indeed inundated with requests but I am bound to say that this is the first time we have been asked to provide a 'dawn chorus'.

After careful consideration of the logistical implications of such a venture, and the possibility that your neighbours may not greet the musical offering with quite the same degree of enthusiasm as yourself, despite the very tempting offer of coffee and croissants I am afraid that we will have to refuse.

As an alternative, may I suggest that you acquire recordings of the choir and set one track up to begin playing at 7am - that way you could ring the changes from day to day, even introducing a seasonal touch at Christmas time. Or as a last resort, you might be able to find a local choir - I believe there is a Choral Society in Huddersfield itself.

With many thanks and best wishes,

As ever,

Professor Ian Tracey
Chorus Master

Philharmonic Hall
Hope Street, Liverpool L1 9BP

Telephone +44(0)151 210 2895
Facsimile +44(0)151 210 2902
Box Office +44(0)151 709 3789

ISDN +44(0)151 709 8746
info@liverpoolphil.com
www.liverpoolphil.com

Patron **Her Majesty the Queen**
Music Director **Gerard Schwarz**
Chairman **Professor Peter Toyne**
Chief Executive **Michael Elliott**

Royal Liverpool Philharmonic Society
Founded 1840
A company limited by guarantee
Registered in England number 88235
Charity number 230538

The Head Chef
The Savoy
The Strand
London WC2R 0EU

Dear Sir

I am writing to you as part of my quest for an unusual item; namely information about purchasing some rare and specific types of food for my forthcoming Roman Toga Party.

As an accomplished and creative chef, I thought that you would be a good starting point for my enquiries and will perhaps be able to throw some light on the supply of some of the commodities described below.

Ever since leaving grammar school almost 25 years ago in the days when Latin and Roman Civilisation were, quite rightly, part of the syllabus, I have been fascinated by the cuisine and delicacies of the ancient world. This partly explains my motives for organising a toga party here in Huddersfield and also for seeking to set out a banquet that would do justice even to the palates of emperors and kings. It is in this respect that I would be grateful for your help and advice.

I thought that it would be a good idea to begin my Roman era entertainment with a selection of dormice dipped in honey, larks' tongues marinated in olive oil and pearls dissolved in vinegar, all of which I have read about in various history books. This will be followed by a choice of refreshing sea-urchin soufflé or rabbit-testicle soup accompanied by a good-quality Chianti wine.

In the tradition of the Emperor Caligula, this lavish feast of extravagance and culinary excellence will then proceed to a main course beyond belief; a whole roasted donkey stuffed with apples and grapes with parsnips in its ears, set upon a silver-plated platter. There will doubtless also be copious amounts of red Italian wines available at this stage as well as a light side salad.

I am not sure whether my guests will have very much room left for a dessert after this meal with a difference but I will nevertheless supply ice-cream, just in case. Plain strawberry will probably suffice.

It is with respect to the purchase of these ancient, mouth-watering and nutritional foodstuffs that I write. I am not sure whether I might be able to find most of the above in a typical supermarket delicatessen or pre-packed foreign meals section or whether I might need to search further afield.

. . . continued

I dare say you deal with enquiries such as mine on a regular basis, and so may I say many thanks indeed for your time and kind consideration. I look forward to hearing from you in the very near future with appropriate advice and helpful suggestions if convenient.

Sincerely

M. A. Lee

Michael A. Lee

SAVOY
LONDON

Mr M A Lee
Somewhere in West Yorkshire

The Savoy
Strand, London WC2R OEU
Telephone (020) 7836 4343
Facsimile (020) 7240 6040
E-mail info@the-savoy.co.uk
Web site www.savoy-group.co.uk

Reservations
Telephone (020) 7420 2500
Facsimile (020) 7872 8901

15th July 2002

Dear Michael,

Thank you for recent letter dated 7th July.

Unfortunately I am due to go on holiday in the next few days and would not have the time to give you the exact details that you are after.

But I do know the difficulty of designing menus for all kinds of occasions. I can therefore recommend a very useful book called 'The Book of Ingredients' by Phillip Dowell and Adrian Bailey.

I hope that this is some use to you and good luck for your event!

Warmest regards and wishes,

Anton Edelmann
Maître Chef des Cuisine

The Savoy Hotel Ltd
Registered in England
No. 3669255
Registered Office
1 Savoy Hill
London WC2R OBP

Somewhere in West Yorkshire
9 July 2002

Head of Customer Services
London Art Co UK Ltd
44 Deepdene Road
London SE5 8EG

Dear Sir/Madam

I am writing to you as part of my quest for an unusual item; namely a 'picture of health'.

Aged 42, I have just began to reach that stage of life where, after many years of cross-country and fell running, my knees creak in a most terrible fashion and my back is as stiff as a board each and every morning.

Whether stress is partly to blame or whether it has more to do with the ravages of age I am not sure, but I am now also as bald as the proverbial coot and possess a face like a dried out wash-leather.

I have far less energy than I did twenty years ago, sleep less predictably and rarely feel refreshed as I go about my daily duties at home and at work. I am pasty, slightly overweight and suffer from perpetual rhinitis and blocked sinuses. To top it all, my friends and family have begun to suggest that I should not smile at people who do not know me lest they become anxious or even frightened. It is for these reasons that I am writing to you.

If you could supply me with a picture that features the face and figure of someone who represents the antithesis of myself, I could hang it on my bedroom wall as if it were a mirror. Perhaps if I were to look at the depiction of someone blessed with good looks and a youthful physique on a regular basis I might begin to gain a new self-image that just could have a beneficial effect on my present state.

If it is true that 'you are what you eat' and 'you are as young as you feel', there may be some truth in the proposition that 'you become what you look at', and an appropriate 'picture of health' might revolutionise my appearance and indeed, my lifestyle.

Since I have tried and been disappointed with most of the alternative methods with supposedly proven rejuvenating abilities, such as eating prunes and cabbage for breakfast, chanting ancient Sumerian incantations and hanging upside down from my landing banisters I decided it was time to move on to more likely options. I would value your advice enormously.

I have no doubts that you receive many requests of this kind on a regular basis and so I thank you for your time and kind consideration and look forward to hearing from you in the near future.

Sincerely

Michael A. Lee

www.londonart.co.uk

London Art Co UK Ltd
24 Deepdene Road
London
SE5 8EG
Tel: 020 7738 3867
Mobile 07711 952808
e-mail: paul.wynter@londonart.co.uk
www.londonart.co.uk

Mr M A Lee
Somewhere in West Yorkshire

19th July, 2002

Dear Michael,

Thanks for your letter, I scan sympathize with much of it, especially the blocked sinuses. Having hit 40 myself this year and with three kids to chase around - life certainly does not get any easier.

I'd love to help find someone to paint your portrait, Most of our Artists like to work from photographs so a sitting may not be necessary. Two that spring to mind are **Escha Van Den Bogerd** and **Alan Graham Dick**. Escha lives in Holland (so only works from photographs) she creates wonderful abstract backgrounds and does seem to flatter her subjects, she's also not expensive at between £340 and £600 depending on what sort of size you would like. Alan has painted some wonderful portraits of some of our clients, he also works from photographs but insists on taking them himself, he's Scottish and older so may well sympathize with your needs. He is however much more expensive as he's relatively well known, his fees are between £1,600 and £6,800.

Do let me know your email address and I would be delighted to send you some sample images of their work. They can of course be found on our website.

Haven't sent a letter in years.

Best wishes

Paul Wynter
Managing Director.

Registration no 3373771, Registered office; 187 High Street, Tonbridge, Kent, TN9 1BX.
VAT no 730705655

**Head of Customer Services
Shoenet
17 Manderwell Road
Oadby
Leicester LE2 5LR**

Dear Sir/Madam

I am writing to you as part of my quest for an unusual item; namely some advice and perhaps even evidence regarding the survival of shoes after their physical demise.

On the basis that shoes have souls I recently began to wonder whether, after their heels have worn down, their leather or other material uppers have become hopelessly thin and the time has arrived for their departure to the bin, they actually make a spiritual transformation into a different dimension.

Surely it is conceivable that the innumerable items of footwear that have provided their wearers with practical and comfortable service over the years might, as their laces are undone one last time, cross the boundaries of life as we know it and travel to a so-called shoe heaven?!

On this basis, I wondered if you might have any information about occasions when owners of a particularly well-loved pair of brogues or suede shoes, slippers or snakeskin boots, have experienced anything like a paranormal event when the time has come for the disposal of their footwear. Such events may well have been reported by refuse collectors or those who scour skips and tips for used bargains.

Have there, for example, been documented cases of people returning home from work to see the ghostly shape of their previously owned slip-ons sitting happily beneath the telephone table where they were always to be found before they fell apart and were thrown on the November bonfire?

Are there any occasions when objects have been kicked mysteriously around a house as if a pair of jealous working boots, ousted from the home many months earlier, were communicating their outrage at the appearance of a pair of new and adequate successors?

Could it be that the tongues we once thought permanently irreparable are actually wagging throughout eternity and the eyelets we considered closed for threading as open in their new dimension as the day they were made?

Doubtless you will receive many enquiries such as this and so I thank you for your time and consideration and look forward to hearing from you in the very near future.

Sincerely

Michael A. Lee

Livingston & Doughty Ltd. _Inc. ShoeNet_

17 Mandervell Road
Oadby
Leicester
_LE2 5LR_

Mr M A Lee   16th July 2002.
Somewhere in West Yorkshire

Dear Mr. Lee,

    We thank you for your letter of 14th July 2002 but regret
that we cannot help you as we have no evidence of the survival of shoes
in the after-life!

    However, we have some fine shoes on our Website and hope that
you will purchase a pair to give you lasting satisfaction in this life!

          Yours sincerely,
        for LIVINGSTON & DOUGHTY LTD.

Managing Director.

WORLDWIDE SUPPLIERS TO THE SHOE INDUSTRY _Registered in England 80205_
Telephone: 44(0)116 271 4221   Fax: 44(0)116 271 6977   E-mail: orders@shoenet.co.uk
Established over one hundred years

Somewhere in West Yorkshire
6 August 2002

Head of Customer Services
Aqualisa Products Ltd
The Flyer's Way
Westerham
Kent TN16 1DE

Dear Sir/Madam

I am writing to you as part of my quest for an unusual item; namely a shower head with a full complement of hair.

Having recently returned from northern France where I spent a rather relaxing two weeks with my family on our annual holiday, it occurred to me that the shower head I used in the bathroom of our rented holiday cottage, like most of the shower heads I have used at home, at the houses of friends and in hotels, was, in effect 'bald'.

If it were not that I am also as bald as the proverbial coot I do not suppose that such follically challenged shower heads would cause me particular concern. But since I am, I frequently note with great anxiety that looking at round, shiny, hairless shower heads during my daily ablutions reminds me of my own ageing state and creates a significant sense of anguish and sadness within the very depths of my being.

It is for this reason that I write to you as a well-established and well-known purveyor of shower-related hardware. If anyone can help me I am convinced it will be you. I would be most grateful, therefore, if you could advice me regarding the availability of alternative shower heads that possess a jolly good head of hair.

Although as a child my own hair was ginger in colour, with a tendency to wave a little when long, I am actually quite flexible when it comes to the colour and style of shower head hair if the current range is restricted. Indeed, a curly Afro-style shower head would be as acceptable to me as one modelling a longer, straighter hippy look, provided the item in question is fully functional and its bare top is completely hidden.

Doubtless you receive many requests along similar lines to this and so I thank you for your time and kind consideration and look forward to hearing from you with appropriate advice in the very near future.

Sincerely

Michael A. Lee

P.S. Do you also provide hats for shower heads in order to keep the hairy ones dry when in use?

AQUALISA PRODUCTS LIMITED
THE FLYER'S WAY · WESTERHAM · KENT TN16 1DE · TELEPHONE: (01959) 560000 · FAX: (01959) 560009
www.aqualisa.co.uk

12th August 2002

Mr M A Lee
Somewhere in West Yorkshire

Dear Mr Lee

Thank you for your letter of 6th August 2002.

Your quest is indeed unusual. As you indicate in your letter, we are a well established manufacturer and supplier of showering products and certainly not a hair today gone tomorrow business. However, our range does not currently contain hairy showers. To be brutally frank, it is not an option for which we have much demand.

I enclose a copy of our current product brochure. These are all of the bald variety although you may find something there you like. If not, may I suggest a wig shop?

Yours sincerely

Marj Brown

Martyn Brown
Customer Service Manager

Enc

Registered Office: Pentagon House, Sir Frank Whittle Road, Derby DE21 4XA   Registered in England No. 1281596
Ultimate Holding Company   Baxi Group Ltd

Customer Service Manager
Furniture 123 Ltd
Sandway Business Centre
Shannon Street
Leeds LS9 8SS

Dear Sir/Madam

I am writing to you as part of my quest for an unusual item; namely the traditional 'ducking stool' that I read about in a recent magazine article on rebellious and awkward wives. As a well-established supplier of various types of stools, I thought that you would be the ideal organisation to which I could write as a useful starting point.

My reference books tell me that the 'ducking stool' was used widely in centuries past as a chair on which disorderly women were seated and subsequently ducked beneath the waters of a pond or lake as suitable punishment for breaking rules and regulations and presenting themselves as trouble-makers and nuisances.

When I read about this superb piece of furniture I immediately decided that life would never again be complete for me without a similar item for use when my own wife is giving me grief and will not toe the line. This happens regularly!

I would be most grateful therefore if you could send details to me of your full range of 'ducking stools' and any literature you might have on strapping and restraining techniques associated with ensuring those seated in these wonderful pieces of ancient woodcraft cannot escape from their deserved and educational submersions.

Many thanks indeed for your time and consideration and I look forward to hearing from you in the very near future.

Sincerely

M. A. Lee

Michael A. Lee

...the home of furniture online

Date: 16/08/2002

Our ref. enquiry

Mr M A Lee
Somewhere in West Yorkshire

Dear Mr Lee

Thank you for you letter dated 14th August. I have had a look through our website and our manufacturers catalogues and I'm afraid we don't have anything resembling a Ducking stool.

I guess we all have a use for such an item at some time or other so if you do find one please let us know!

Best of luck.

Kind Regards

Jonathan Seal
Customer Services Manager
Furniture 123 Ltd.

Furniture 123 Ltd, Sandway Business Centre, Shannon Street, Leeds LS9 8SS
Tel: 0113 248 2233 Fax: 0113 248 2266 Email: info@furniture123.co.uk Website: www.furniture123.co.uk
Registered in England and Wales. Company No 2696994

Somewhere in West Yorkshire
14 August 2002

Head of English
The University of Bradford
Bradford
West Yorkshire

Dear Sir/Madam

I am writing to you as part of my quest for an unusual item; namely some advice regarding a course of study that might lead to a 'Degree of Comparison' and the possibility of undertaking this at the prestigious University of Bradford.

Ever since I was a small boy I have been interested in comparing the various merits, dimensions and characteristics of innumerable items, objects and creatures within the animal, vegetable and mineral worlds. Had I lived in ancient times I am convinced I would have been the man who invented the vast grammatical array of comparative terms such as 'smaller', 'wider' and 'a great deal more purple' and might well have held the noble title of 'State Comparitor'.

Relative to many of my peers – there I go again – I would estimate my ability at assessing the relation between the majority of things as better than most and at least as good as the remainder. In addition to this long-established skill of objective assessment, that I trust will assure you of my ideal candidacy for the aforementioned degree course, I also have a swimming certificate showing my adequacy at completing a full length in a modern pool. This is surely a more worthy accomplishment than a mere width though admittedly not quite as good as a quarter mile!

Doubtless there will be great interest from many quarters in accessing a course leading to a 'Degree of Comparison' and so I thank you for your time and kind consideration.

I look forward to hearing from you in the very near future.

Sincerely

Michael A. Lee

UNIVERSITY OF BRADFORD

16th August 2002

Mr M A Lee
Somewhere in West Yorkshire

Dear Mr Lee

Your letter of 14th August addressed to the 'Head of English' was delivered to the Language Unit.

I am not sure if we can help you in your quest. Your letter was stranger than many I have seen during my time in the university but not as odd as some.

It will probably come as no surprise that the University of Bradford does not run a 'Degree of Comparison' with the entry requirement of a swimming certificate. However, I am enclosing the current prospectus for the School of Lifelong Education and Development as you may be interested in taking some of the modules offered. You may find some better than others.

Yours sincerely

Elspeth Allcock
Administrator

Lang/comparison
UNIVERSITY OF BRADFORD   WEST YORKSHIRE   BD7 1DP   UK
TEL +44 (0)1274 235208/234578   FAX +44 (0)1274 235207
EMAIL langunit@bradford.ac.uk.   www.bradford.ac.uk/acad/langunit

MAKING
KNOWLEDGE
WORK

Somewhere in West Yorkshire
8 September 2002

Head of Customer Services
Dickinson & Morris Ltd
Ye Olde Pork Pie Shoppe
8–10 Nottingham Street
Melton Mowbray
Leicestershire LE13 1NW

Dear Sir/Madam

I am writing to you as part of my quest for an unusual item; namely a substantial supply of 'humble pie'.

Only yesterday my dear wife confronted me after an episode of disagreement around evening meal arrangements, looked straight into my eyes and suggested that I should eat a large portion of 'humble pie'.

To be perfectly frank with you I am not sure whether she was worried that I am not eating sufficiently well at present or whether she thought that a bite of something tasty and nutritious might compensate for our angry words and differences in opinion and thus ameliorate my negative mood.

It is in this regard, therefore, that I am writing to you as a well-established manufacturer and purveyor of pies in an attempt to order the aforementioned pie for consumption as soon as is conveniently possible, assuming, of course, that this type of pie features within your product range.

Although I have seen many, many varieties of pork pie, game pie and indeed apple pie, I have never actually seen or tasted a humble pie and would, as a consequence, be most grateful for your advice and suggestions regards obtaining such.

Doubtless you receive innumerable letters of a similar nature to this and so I am most grateful for your time and kind consideration and I look forward to hearing from you in the very near future.

Sincerely

Michael A. Lee

DICKINSON & MORRIS

ADMINISTRATION

PO BOX 580

LEICESTER LE4 1ZN

TELEPHONE (0116) 235 5900

FAX (0116) 235 5711

E-MAIL dickinson&morris@porkpie.co.uk

www.porkpie.co.uk

DICKINSON & MORRIS

8 - 10 NOTTINGHAM STREET

MELTON MOWBRAY

LEICESTERSHIRE

ENGLAND LE13 1NW

TELEPHONE (01664) 562341

FAX (01664) 568052

Mr M A Lee
Somewhere in West Yorkshire

11th September 2002

Dear Mr Lee,

I am in receipt of your recent letter regarding whether or not we have "humble" pies within our product portfolio.

At Dickinson & Morris we produce not only the Rolls Royce equivalent of pork pies, but probably the finest pork pie in the world. Dickinson & Morris have been baking and selling this delicious English delicacy from Ye Olde Pork Pie Shoppe, in Melton Mowbray, since 1851. Our pies are made with hand-trimmed shoulder and belly of fresh, British pork, seasoned with traditional spices, encased and hand-crimped in a hot water pastry, baked until golden and then jellied with a natural pork bone stock. The resultant pie is a glorious combination of tasty and succulent pork with a rich and crunchy crust.

We therefore think that this would make it a good contender for a "humble" pie, being nutritious, satisfying and excellent value for money. I have enclosed a copy our brochure, should you wish to sample one.

Yours sincerely,

ANDREA TOMLIN
BRAND MANAGER

BORN AND RAISED IN MELTON MOWBRAY

REGISTERED OFFICE: CHETWODE HOUSE, LEICESTER ROAD, MELTON MOWBRAY, LEICESTERSHIRE. LE13 1GA. REGISTERED NO. 03116767 ENGLAND

Dickinson & Morris is a division of Samworth Brothers Limited.

Samworth Brothers

EPILOGUE

It is with a certain degree of light-hearted disappointment that I must tell you of my abject failure in acquiring a single specific product, title or membership as a consequence of my many letters written late at night and with much earnestness.

Although those who have replied have done so with great thought and sensitivity, humour and goodwill, good manners and cultured courtesy, I have received not a single chocolate teapot in my written quest for a most unusual item.

Alas, there are those who did not have the heart to reply to me in the first instance and so in some cases – such as the pursuit of work 'Pyramid Selling' from the British Ambassador at our embassy in Egypt – my search was thwarted without even a basic explanation of refusal.

However, there is always a silver lining in the darkest of clouds, a ray of hope in the dingiest of dungeons and water beneath the sands of perceived desert wastelands. In collecting together the myriad letters and replies that comprise my quest I have acquired the material for this book. Granted, there is nothing unusual about books *per se*. But perhaps you will agree that this book is a very unusual one indeed and so my quest for an unusual item has been serendipitously satisfied, and I might now rest awhile by the fire looking to the dancing flames for warmth and yet more inspiration as the winter winds howl outside and my readers wonder whether anyone ever did find the real Cloud Cuckoo Land.

ACKNOWLEDGEMENTS

Without the patient and consistent support of my understanding wife, Ann-Marie, and my two energetic sons, Tom and George, I doubt that I would have found the time and ability to complete this, my second book, in a little over six months. Thank you. Fine Belgian chocolates will be eaten, champagne poured and consumed with great relish and a band hired forthwith. (I also intend to sort something out for the three of you!)

Thanks too to my Mum and Dad who convinced me on innumerable occasions during my childhood and throughout my teenage years that to speak and write English in this great land of England is an invaluable asset. You were right.

I would also like to thank a number of people for their encouragement along the way, including Melanie Letts, Jeremy Robson and the rest of the team at Robson Books, Eamon and Fran McGoldrick, Rob and Annika Acheson, Pete Faulkner, Steve Hemingway, Mike Fleming, Andy and Janet Hodgson, Richard and Sarah Lee, Graham and Suzanne Almack, Garry Taylor, Jim Sedgeley, John Kimberley and the many readers of my first book who requested a second compilation.

Here also is tribute to the late but great Spike Milligan whose off-the-wall humour has amused and inspired me for years, and to the gifted Michael Palin for his support of my walk on the lateral side of life.

When my first book, *Written in Jest*, was published in November 2002 I was invited to spend a little time in the Bodmin Moor area where I was officially inaugurated as 'The Beast of Bodmin Moor'. I enjoyed a most welcome break; it was a short but inspirational period of time. I would therefore like to recognise the Bodmin Moor area and the talented local business people who have formed The Best of Bodmin Moor Marketing Group, for being instrumental in my persevering with this, my second book of constructed lunacy and collected humour.

I raise my glass to Jeremy and Collette Capper of Mount Pleasant Farm (with their most comfortable holiday cottages) and to the rest of the Bodmin gang for encouragement along the way. I would ask my readers to check out their fascinating website at www.bodminmoor.co.uk.

Finally, here's to you all and thank you for purchasing and taking the time to read this book. Should you wish to learn a little more about the first book, please visit my website at www.written-in-jest.co.uk.